C000117889

HI
A PRISON PRAYER BOOK

Published by Augsburg Fortress

Hear My Voice: A Prison Prayer Book

See the Acknowledgments on page 231 for details about
materials that are derived from other sources.

Printed in U.S.A.
ISBN 978-1-5064-4960-9

22 21   3 4 5 6 7 8 9 10

CONTENTS

Additional Ways to Pray

Scripture and Song

Appendixes

Yearning for God

O Lord, hear my voice!

—Psalm 130:2

INVITATION
INTO PRAYER

WELCOME TO THIS RESOURCE

The title of this book, *Hear My Voice* (Psalm 130:2), is itself a prayer for difficult times. It can be a plea: "Please, God, hear me!" It can be a challenge: "OK, God, if you're really there, then listen to me!" It can be a cry of faith: "I know that you're with me, Jesus, and that you'll hear my voice when I call to you." And it is, at the same time, *God's* invitation to each of us. God says, "Hear *my* voice," because God is always listening for our prayers and ready to respond.

What This Book Is About

This book is about praying to God and listening for God in prison. God is present in prison—after all, Jesus was condemned by the religious authorities of his day and arrested and executed by the Roman state. Many of Jesus' followers through the centuries have faced imprisonment. So, prisons are outposts of heaven. They are places where the Holy Spirit is present and active, transforming lives and situations. Jesus Christ is on our side and by our side, no matter what hardships or challenges or enemies we face—including incarceration.

The brutal realities of this world often seem disconnected from God's love and justice. Yet, God's justice is the deeper truth. God's justice is about grace, forgiveness, hope, and new life. It is about restoring broken relationships and healing shattered hearts. God's justice is respect, fairness, and safety for every person. The penal system keeps people separated and apart. But God's vision for us is connection with Christ and one another, even when we sit in solitude or in solitary confinement.

Who This Book Is For
If you currently live in a prison, this book may help you deepen your walk with God. We hope it will be a companion for you as you live out your Christian faith on the inside. The writers of this book are currently or have been incarcerated or involved in prison or re-entry ministries. Hear *our* voices praying for you and with you.

If you are a family member or friend of someone who is incarcerated, you may find this book helpful. Use it to pray alongside your loved one, even though you are physically separated.

This book is also a call to the church and to every congregation to be in prayer and solidarity with people who are incarcerated. Jesus says that whenever we visit someone in prison, we visit him (Matthew 25:36, 40). We hope this book helps connect those inside prison with those outside, and those outside with those inside. We offer it in Jesus' name to all who may find it useful.

How to Use This Prayer Book

The prayers and liturgies here can be prayed alone in a jail cell or in a small group on the cell block. The seasons in the "Praying through the Year" section journey with Jesus over the course of the year from his birth through his ministry to his death and resurrection. "Praying through Ordinary Days" invites us into deepening friendship with Christ amid the realities of life in prison. Prayer patterns for morning and evening offer ways to pray throughout the day. The devotional practices offered in the rest of the book are suggestions to spark creativity in prayer. And the artwork offers a vision of God's creative Spirit at work in each of us.

We want to honor the privacy of those who have shared their stories and experiences here. Therefore, throughout this book, all names of those in prison have been changed.

May the Spirit be with you, may Christ sustain you, and may God guide you every moment of every day. God says, "Hear my voice":

"Do not be afraid."
  "I am with you."
    "I will help you."
      "I have called you by name."
        "You are my beloved child."
          "Come as you are and know that I am God."
            "I will never leave you or forsake you."

WHY DO TIME IN PRAYER?

In a system full of rejection and short on compassion, we want you to see yourself as God sees you, and to know deep in your bones that God delights in you. God loves you unconditionally! The most basic way for any of us to receive God's deep and constant love is through the practice of prayer.

Prayer is the name we give to both listening for and responding to the voice of God, which is always speaking love to us, though we sometimes can't hear it. The problem is that the voice we often hear—the voice we're trained to hear—is a voice of rejection. Rejection and condemnation are the stock-in-trade of the prison system. So, chances are that this is the voice ringing in your ears and echoing in your soul. Of course, a person doesn't have to go through the prison system to be bombarded by this voice. It recaps all our missteps and regrets and proclaims, loud and clear, the false conclusions of a broken system: It says we're no good. It says we're of no value. It says we've ruined everything. Tragically, we often assume this is the voice of God.

It is *not!*

Rather, it is the voice of the Accuser. The Accuser is like a prosecuting attorney hammering away at all that we have done wrong to try to convince us to condemn ourselves. This voice drives us to a place of shame where self-condemnation isolates us from the love and community for which God created us.

But there is another voice. It is the true voice of God, who never condemns or disqualifies us. It is the voice that raises us from shame and self-hatred to our true stature as beloved children of God. Listening to and trusting God's voice dispels the voice of the Accuser within us. Jesus calls the voice of God—this Spirit of God—the "Advocate." This Advocate stands by us constantly to remind us who we are in the eyes of God: beloved children, and heirs to the kingdom of heaven. This Advocate is the Spirit of Jesus himself, who champions the truth that we are God's beloved. Yes, we may have done bad things. Yes, we may have made bad decisions and may be guilty of many wrongs. God knows! But the Advocate, the Spirit of Jesus, defends us from condemnation.

For the Advocate, it's never about "guilty or innocent." It's about who we are before God. This voice insists that what we have done does not define us. What we have done cannot disqualify us from the love of God. When we begin to hear the voice of God, the lies we have heard over and over about ourselves slowly come to light. The isolating shame starts to dissolve. And our soul begins to sense the loving connection we have with God and our neighbors.

Prayer re-tunes the ear and the soul to listen to and trust the voice of God. This discipline takes practice and includes many kinds of prayer. This book is a guide for that practice.

You might be tempted to think you have to feel a certain way when you begin to pray. Not so. As you begin (or continue) to explore prayer, you will find yourself somewhere on a long continuum of experience that stretches from ecstasy to comfortable familiarity to awkwardness to boredom. Here's the thing: any place on the prayer-experience spectrum is a great place to be because God is *everywhere* on that spectrum! God will meet us wherever we are in order to enter into a relationship with us. This loving connection with God is the important thing to keep in mind.

Another temptation might be to think you have to master *all* these prayer practices. Far from it! Thomas Merton, a twentieth-century mystic, said of prayer, "We will never be anything but beginners, all our life!!"[1] So we never need to worry about "mastering" any one prayer, let alone all the prayers in this resource. There are many ways to pray, and not all kinds of prayer will be helpful for everyone. Still, there are prayer practices for everyone. We invite you to explore the many styles of prayer offered here and find the kinds of prayer that speak most profoundly to you. The rule of thumb is to pray as you are able and let the loving connection with God be your guide into the practices of prayer.

We suggest a simple first step: Find a short, simple prayer in this book. Begin to say it over and over. Such a practice will start to quiet the accusing voice and still your mind. Inevitably, the Accuser will try to regain your ear. However, little by little, you will hear and call forth the Advocate, who will continually replace the accusing voice with the voice of God. The voice of truth will echo in your ear and soul: "You are my beloved. In you I take delight!"

PRAYING THROUGH THE YEAR

THE SEASONS OF THE CHURCH YEAR

This chapter invites you to experience the cycle of the Christian year, which follows the life of Jesus Christ our Lord. The church calendar is different from the secular calendar. The dates of most of the major events change each year, depending on the cycles of the moon. You'll find a handy chart in the back of this book listing the dates for Advent, Ash Wednesday, Easter, and Pentecost for the next thirty years (see page 230).

The *Advent* season begins the Christian year. It starts four Sundays before December 25. It is a four-week period to prepare ourselves for Jesus' birth at Christmas and for his promised return in glory at the end of time.

Christmas, December 25, is the day we celebrate the birth of Jesus, when God came among us as a human being. In the church, the celebration of Christmas continues for twelve days.

The day of *Epiphany* falls on January 6. During the weeks of the Epiphany season, we recall the events of

Jesus' childhood, especially the journey of the wise men who followed the star to Bethlehem to see Jesus, who is the light of the world. We also remember his baptism and early ministry.

The season of **Lent** begins with **Ash Wednesday** and lasts for forty days. In Lent we focus on Jesus' final journey to Jerusalem. We also consider our own life journey of repentance, hope, and change.

During **Holy Week**, we remember Jesus' arrival in Jerusalem on **Palm Sunday**, his final meal with his disciples (the Last Supper) on **Maundy Thursday**, and his betrayal, arrest, trial, conviction, and execution on **Good Friday**.

On **Easter** Sunday we celebrate the resurrection— that God raised Jesus from the dead. This is the most important event of the Christian faith, so for Christians, every Sunday since that first Easter is a celebration of Easter. The Easter season lasts for fifty days.

Pentecost Sunday comes fifty days after Easter Sunday. It is the celebration of the coming of the Holy Spirit and the beginning of the Christian church. The season after Pentecost stretches through the rest of the year until Advent comes around again. Throughout this time, Christians follow the gospel stories of the life and ministry of Jesus and seek the guidance of the Holy Spirit.

My Soul Magnifies the Lord

Wait for the Lord, and be strong.
Take heart and wait for the Lord!

—*Psalm 27:14*

How to Use This Section

This part of the book offers resources to help you pray your way through the seasons of the church year with your Christian siblings around the globe. Just start with whichever season of the church year you're in now. The chart in the back of the book (page 230) may help you determine that. Each seasonal piece begins with a short mantra-type prayer. These prayers can be said over and over to help you focus your thoughts on God throughout the day. Then spend time pondering the scripture passage and reflection for the day. The quotations offer insights to think about. The questions are intended to spark your own thoughts and prayers on the theme of the day. You may wish to pray the longer prayer and sing the song to end your prayer time. If the song isn't familiar to you, you might just pray it as a prayer-poem. Or feel free to choose your own song or to make up your own melodies to go with the words—just "make a joyful noise to the LORD!" (Psalm 100:1).

WHAT DO YOU WAIT FOR? ADVENT

Mantra Prayer
Wait with me, Lord. Guide my hope, tame my fear.

Scripture for Advent: Luke 1:39-44, 46-56
In those days Mary set out and went with haste to a Judean town in the hill country, where she entered the house of Zechariah and greeted Elizabeth. When Elizabeth heard Mary's greeting, the child leaped in her womb. And Elizabeth was filled with the Holy Spirit and exclaimed with a loud cry, "Blessed are you among women, and blessed is the fruit of your womb. And why has this happened to me, that the mother of my Lord comes to me? For as soon as I heard the sound of your greeting, the child in my womb leaped for joy."

And Mary said, "My soul magnifies the Lord, and my spirit rejoices in God my Savior, for he has looked with favor on the lowliness of his servant. Surely, from now on all generations will call me blessed; for the Mighty One has done great things for me, and holy is his name. His mercy is for those who fear him from generation to generation. He has shown strength with his arm; he has scattered the proud in the thoughts of their hearts. He has brought down the powerful from their thrones, and lifted up the lowly; he has filled the hungry with good things, and sent the rich away empty. He has helped his servant Israel, in remembrance of his mercy, according to the promise he made to our ancestors, to Abraham and to his descendants forever." And Mary remained with her about three months and then returned to her home.

Reflection

I began collecting "waiting stories" in the prison where I was living. When I asked several inmates the question "What do you wait for?" nearly every one of them gave me a puzzled look of disinterested mockery, signaling irritation. "What kind of stupid question is that? It's all about waiting. Prison is all about waiting. That's what we do here." But I persisted.

A lot of what they told me was predictable: I wait for mail, for a visit, for count, for library time, recreation time, meal time, canteen time ... for the lawyer to call, the judge to decide, the committee to meet ... for anything that will break the wretched, numbing boredom. For release!

Still, the more I asked, and the longer the inmates talked about waiting, the more I heard unexpected, soulful words. Words like *forgiveness, choices, worth, respect, meaning, hope, touch, love*. They were words that, for all their different consonants and vowels and syllables, sounded like the word "mercy."

Advent means "coming." If one word or one mood describes Advent, it might well be waiting. But waiting for what? Waiting is one part hope and another part fear; it can be a measure of wanting and a dose of dread. To encourage us in our waiting, we'll explore this revolutionary passage about Mary and Elizabeth throughout this Advent section, as a companion for our question "What do you wait for?"

A Quote to Ponder
Above all, trust in the slow work of God. We are, quite naturally, impatient in everything to reach the end without delay. —Pierre Teilhard de Chardin[2]

A Question to Wonder About
What do you wait for?

Song
Canticle of the Turning

> My soul cries out with a joyful shout
> that the God of my heart is great,
> and my spirit sings of the wondrous things
> that you bring to the ones who wait.
> You fixed your sight on your servant's plight,
> and my weakness you did not spurn,
> so from east to west shall my name be blest.
> Could the world be about to turn?
>
> My heart shall sing of the day you bring.
> Let the fires of your justice burn.
> Wipe away all tears, for the dawn draws near,
> and the world is about to turn.
> Rory Cooney, b. 1952, based on the Magnificat[3]

ADVENT 1: SOME KIND OF LONGING

Mantra Prayer
Wait with me, Lord. Do not turn away; stay with me now.

Scripture: Luke 1:39-45
In those days Mary set out and went with haste to a Judean town in the hill country, where she entered the house of Zechariah and greeted Elizabeth. When Elizabeth heard Mary's greeting, the child leaped in her womb. And Elizabeth was filled with the Holy Spirit and exclaimed with a loud cry, "Blessed are you among women, and blessed is the fruit of your womb. And why has this happened to me, that the mother of my Lord comes to me? For as soon as I heard the sound of your greeting, the child in my womb leaped for joy. And blessed is she who believed that there would be a fulfillment of what was spoken to her by the Lord."

Reflection
Sentenced to twenty-five years when he was just nineteen, Montal had fourteen years left when I met him. When he showed me a greeting card from his mother, he told me she'd not been to see him in a decade. Rob was shocked by a surprise visit from his brother and cried for as many reasons as their years lived apart. Jess's voice broke as he admitted that his teenage son, angry at having a father in prison, had renounced him and changed his name.

For many in prison, *family* is a bitter word that pokes at painful, unfilled spaces in life. "Family First" tattooed on inmates' forearms—with who knows how many meanings?—reveals some kind of longing. Unaffordable miles of separation, ignored visiting lists, desperation pen-pals, and blocked phone numbers expose lost relationships.

Mary and Elizabeth were cousins. Both unexpectedly pregnant, they each had reason to be frightened. A vulnerable target for ridicule, Mary raced away to Elizabeth with the burden and excitement of her news. She wanted family. She needed the nearness of someone who would understand what so many others could not.

There is no hint in the reading that anyone went along with Mary in her rush to Elizabeth's house. Did no family member care? Was she running away from home or running to family? We can only guess. But what we do know is that both women find themselves waiting: Elizabeth, the old woman who had never been able to have a child (which made her a disgrace to family and community), and Mary, the young woman who was pregnant but not by the man to whom she was engaged (which made her dishonorable to family and community). They wait, not for judgment, but to receive the promise of God's mercy. They wait for a future with hope.

Mary and Elizabeth. Montal, Rob, and Jess. How do they relate to one another? If this Bible story is just about the lives of an old lady and her young cousin long ago, it doesn't much matter. But the story of Mary and Elizabeth is the story of us all. It is the story of anyone who has ever known what it means to be forgotten, rejected, or written off. It is the blessing of God. A God who promises—for reasons that have nothing to do with our own behavior but everything to do with God's goodness—to never not love us. A God who promises always to remain near us, because we are God's own beloved family.

A Quote to Ponder
I don't know anything about it, but the sight of the stars always makes me dream. —Vincent van Gogh[4]

A Question to Wonder About

Where do you find the gift of understanding, and how can you be understanding to others?

Prayer

Never-absent God, you have chosen to come into the world just as I came. You know the joys and the burdens of family, the comfort and loss of friendship, and the need for love. With you near, I remember and name, now, those who love and support me (*especially name*). I pray for healing of the sorrows and wounds of separation and loss. I ask you to bless me with the gift of companionship and understanding. I ask this in the name of Jesus. Amen.

Song

It Came upon the Midnight Clear

> It came upon the midnight clear,
> that glorious song of old,
> from angels bending near the earth
> to touch their harps of gold:
> "Peace on the earth, good will to all,
> from heav'n's all-gracious king."
> The world in solemn stillness lay
> to hear the angels sing.
>
> Edmund H. Sears, 1810–1876

ADVENT 2: SONG FOR THE LOWLY

Mantra Prayer
Wait with me, Lord. Look on me with mercy and compassion.

Scripture: Luke 1:46-48, 50
And Mary said, "My soul magnifies the Lord, and my spirit rejoices in God my Savior, for he has looked with favor on the lowliness of his servant. Surely, from now on all generations will call me blessed.... His mercy is for those who fear him from generation to generation."

Reflection
It was Christmas Eve, just minutes before the six o'clock chapel service. Bible in hand, Joe dashed from his housing unit, rushing under the spray of prison yard floodlights that made the falling snow glisten. It was the kind of Christmas scene made for greeting cards, if you could ignore the razor wire and guard towers. In his hurry to get from one building to another, Joe hadn't pulled the plastic I.D. tag to the outside of his coat where it could be seen. When he arrived at the door, he was met by a guard standing away from the drifting snow. "Where do you think you are going?" "To the chapel service." "No, you're not! I don't see your tag—you must be nobody." The inmate began unzipping his coat to show the guard a purple I.D. strung on a plastic lanyard. "Too late! Tonight, I'm God here, and you're out of luck." Joe stood winter-faced, without words. "Head back to your cell, Mr. Nobody. And Merry Christmas."

Mary knew what it meant to be invisible. That was the reality for most women in her world. But for Mary, the situation must have been especially severe because she lived under the brutal authority of the Roman Empire, which pressed down on its

Jewish subjects with a merciless, heavy hand. It was a culture where justice served the powerful while oppressing the weak.

If anyone thought of her at all, Mary would have been considered lowly. Maybe she even thought it of herself, which makes these lines from Luke all the more remarkable. They are verses of a song—often called "Mary's Song," and also known as the Magnificat. It is the song of a lowly young woman praising God's mercy.

The lowly are all who are denied the blessings in life that God intends all of creation—*all*—to receive. Denied perhaps because of what they have done or failed to do, or where they were born, or their health, or their gender, or their resources or color or intelligence or morals or occupation, or for whatever reason. The lowly are the nameless, the ones reduced to numbers, the "others" in the shadows, so easy to forget.

Mary risked believing that the words she heard from God's messenger, Gabriel, might really be true. She risked believing that God looked upon her with favor, that she needn't be afraid, that there was hope that God would indeed show mercy.

And so, Mary sang her song. She sang for herself and for all of us. She sings of mercy for people overlooked and turned away. She sings for the defeated and the denied. She sings for the guilty and the innocent, the regretful and the despairing. Her song is for the angry, the stuck, the scared, the lonely, the sad. It reverberates among the indigent and the aimless. It echoes from age to eon, from corner to core, repeated in the known and the unknown, over bitter waters, out of harsh winds, into gutting fires. It is a song for each person who waits for God's mercy.

A Quote to Ponder

Hold fast to dreams
For when dreams go
Life is a barren field
Frozen with snow.

—Langston Hughes[5]

A Question to Wonder About

Where are you waiting for God's mercy in your own life?

Prayer

Lowly Lord Jesus, you have known rejection and judgment, been accused and sentenced, disgraced with the lowly and condemned by the mighty. You see where I am and know me as others do not. Watch over me with kindness, free me from shame, and teach me to look at others in mercy. Amen.

Song

Love Divine, All Loves Excelling

> Love divine, all loves excelling,
> Joy of heav'n, to earth come down!
> Fix in us thy humble dwelling,
> all thy faithful mercies crown.
> Jesus, thou art all compassion,
> pure, unbounded love thou art;
> visit us with thy salvation,
> enter ev'ry trembling heart.

Charles Wesley, 1707-1788

ADVENT 3: WHAT GREAT THINGS?

Mantra Prayer
Wait with me, Lord; reveal your greatness, and encourage
my faith.

Scripture: Luke 1:46, 49
And Mary said, "My soul magnifies the Lord ... for the Mighty
One has done great things for me, and holy is his name."

Reflection
I was a brand-new inmate. Everything about life in a cell
was strange and frightening. All the worst stories of what
to expect in prison pressed my spirit flat like iron against
flesh. An officer directed me to the second tier, where a door
buzzed with a steely hiss as it rolled aside for me to pass out
of one life and into another. In that moment, I remembered
an oddly gracious blessing a friend had spoken over me only
days before: "You have lost everything; there is nothing more
for you to lose. Few people have such an unchosen privilege to
begin a new life." A strange blessing indeed.

It took enormous courage, the kind of courage that is willing
to endure ridicule and provoke outrage, for Mary to believe
and to announce brazenly, "The Mighty One has done great
things for me." By most human evidence, she qualified as
unworthy of respect in a world that admires accomplishment
and fortune and pedigree. But Mary believed the promise of
God's word, that she had already received great things from
God! Where did she find the heart for that brave faith?

Behind me, the steel door growled to a close and then clanked
into its lock. There I was, with my unchosen privilege to begin
a new life. An inmate stood inches away by the bunks, ready to

introduce himself: "Hola, mi nombre es Manuel." Within minutes, he offered coffee and a cookie. "Mi madre—my mother," he said, changing his language, "always believed if there is enough for one, there is enough for two. It's true. ¿Sí? That's such a great thing, don't you think?" he said. "¡Bienvenido!"

What great things could Mary look forward to? Her child of promise would be born under wretched circumstances. She, Joseph, and the baby would be targets of a government-sponsored massacre. They would flee by night and become refugees in a foreign land. When they returned home, they would still fear for their lives. When Jesus' ministry began at his hometown synagogue, he would be driven out of town by a mob threatening to kill him. Finally, his young life would end with a state execution while Mary watched, weeping, at the crucifixion.

What great things? This Jesus will show us: He eats with the scandalous. He befriends the thieves. He feeds the hungry. He welcomes the outcasts. He forgives the sinners. He trusts the faithless. And in the end, from behind the door of death where everything seemed lost, new life waited no longer—it began!

A Quote to Ponder
We are told of meek obedience. No one mentions courage.
The engendering Spirit did not enter her without consent.
God waited. —Denise Levertov[6]

A Question to Wonder About
When in the events or moments of these days have you experienced God's unusual, unexpected great things?

Prayer

Holy, mighty God, you reveal the mystery of true greatness. To the frightened and troubled, you give hope. To the guilty and outcast, you give a new day. And among the oppressed and imprisoned, you offer release. Where I see only dead ends, show me a new way. In my fear, lead me to courage. And in my doubts, direct me to faith. With hope, I ask it in the name of Jesus. Amen.

Song

My Soul Proclaims Your Greatness

> My soul proclaims your greatness, Lord;
> I sing my Savior's praise!
> You looked upon my lowliness,
> and I am full of grace.
> Now ev'ry land and ev'ry age
> this blessing shall proclaim—
> great wonders you have done for me,
> and holy is your name.[7]
>
> From Luke 1:46-55

ADVENT 4: SUCH WEIRD STRENGTH

Mantra Prayer

Wait with me, Lord; be my strength for today, my comfort tomorrow.

Scripture: Luke 1:46, 51-53

And Mary said, "...[The Mighty One] has shown strength with his arm; he has scattered the proud in the thoughts of their hearts. He has brought down the powerful from their thrones, and lifted up the lowly; he has filled the hungry with good things, and sent the rich away empty."

Reflection

He grew up on the streets, where carrying a gun preceded puberty, where teen drug deals paid the rent that a long-gone father didn't and bought groceries that his mother couldn't. Where robbery was the rite of initiation and theft the mark of courage. There, strength wears a strange costume. And don't most of us want to be strong—or at least to appear strong? So, he carried the gun, and he used it. He sold dope to have a roof and a bed, he bought cereal and milk and tater tots for his sisters and brother, and he stole Nikes and broke into cars to prove he was strong.

But he wasn't strong enough to admit that he secretly pedaled a bike to the shore of Lake Michigan where he read poetry. Or that he loved to watch silly TV shows with his grandma. Or that he was tired of being hungry. Or that most of the time he was scared. Or that he hurt from the hands that hit him and did worse. Or that he just wanted to be loved. Then he went to prison—a boy who tried to be strong enough not to cry.

Prison has its own weird culture of strength that turns recreation fields and gym floors into combat zones. Where crime stories decorate a person the way Scouts pin on merit badges. Where shouted abuses throb into dayroom phones until time is used up or money runs out. Where secret tears are drained in the shower and soak into pillows. It's a weird strength where "toughen up" treads over "open up" and vengeance ridicules forgiveness. Prison has its own weird culture of strength.

When Mary sings about God's way of showing strength, her words do away with all popular thoughts of what it means to be strong. She lunges into a daring riff about strength shown by mercy toward the hungry and poor and lowly, not by the pride and privilege of the powerful. She sings an introduction to all that the child she carries in her womb will become. Her song is a prelude to Jesus' ministry in which the last will become first, a servant is made master, and the weak are strong.

God looks at the way the world has chosen to spin and flips it into another orbit. God sees the unmerciful rules we have codified for our lives and breaks them, one after another: Blessed are you who are poor, you who are hungry, you who weep, you who are hated, excluded, reviled, defamed. Love your enemies, do good to those who hate you, bless those who curse you, pray for those who abuse you (Luke 6).

And then, after Mary's song, after the waiting, the child would be born, and there would be another song. All the heavens would break open, singing: "Glory to God in the highest heaven, and on earth peace among those whom he favors!" (Luke 2:14).

A Quote to Ponder
A prison cell, in which one waits, hopes, does various unessential things, and is completely dependent on the fact that the door of freedom has to be opened from the outside, is not a bad picture of Advent. —Dietrich Bonhoeffer[8]

A Question to Wonder About
In what ways is strength difficult for you?

Prayer

Just and compassionate God, you provide strength through goodness and show the power of compassion. You lift up those who are down low and promise relief for the poor. Defend me from all violence, provide the courage I need to be kind, assist me in being forgiving, and fill me with the spirit of generosity. I pray this in Jesus' name. Amen.

Song

Comfort, Comfort Now My People

> "Comfort, comfort now my people;
> tell of peace!" So says our God.
> Comfort those who sit in darkness
> mourning under sorrow's load.
> To God's people now proclaim
> that God's pardon waits for them!
> Tell them that their war is over;
> God will reign in peace forever.

Johann G. Olearius, 1635-1711; tr. Catherine Winkworth, 1827-1878, alt.

GOD DWELLING AMONG US: CHRISTMAS

Mantra Prayer

Be still and know that I am God
Be still and know that I am
Be still and know that I
Be still and know that
Be still and know
Be still and
Be still
Be

Scripture: Isaiah 9:4; 6-7

For the yoke of their burden, and the bar across their shoulders, the rod of their oppressor, you have broken as on the day of Midian.... For a child has been born for us, a son given to us; authority rests upon his shoulders; and he is named Wonderful Counselor, Mighty God, Everlasting Father, Prince of Peace. His authority shall grow continually, and there shall be endless peace for the throne of David and his kingdom. He will establish and uphold it with justice and with righteousness from this time onward and forevermore.

Reflection

At long last, our Advent hopes are fulfilled: Christmas has arrived! God's promise for a Savior to rule with peace and justice has come in the form of a newborn baby—Jesus. The vast mystery of God is suddenly embodied in an infant named Jesus, crying out into the world just as each one of us did at our birth.

We call this event—God being born as a human—the Incarnation, meaning God "in the flesh." Although the word *incarnation* looks and sounds similar to the word *incarceration*, the two could not be more opposite. *Incarceration* refers to imprisonment, solitude, and confinement. It is about separating the person from the world. *Incarnation* is God becoming human to walk with us on our earthly journey, to save us, and to set us free.

The best news of this Christmas miracle is that God continues to come into our hearts and meet us wherever we are. Prison walls can't keep God out. In fact, the Bible says that "neither death, nor life, nor angels, nor rulers, nor things present, nor things to come, nor powers, nor height, nor depth, nor anything else in all creation, will be able to separate us from the love of God in Christ Jesus our Lord" (Romans 8:38-39).

A Quote to Ponder

Christmas did not come after a great mass of people had completed something good, or because of the successful result of any human effort. No, it came as a miracle, as the child that comes when his time is fulfilled, as a gift. —Eberhard Arnold[9]

A Question to Wonder About

What does the fulfillment of God's promise mean to you?

Song

Go Tell It on the Mountain

> Go tell it on the mountain, over the hills and ev'rywhere;
> go tell it on the mountain that Jesus Christ is born!
>
> While shepherds kept their watching
> o'er silent flocks by night,
> behold, throughout the heavens
> there shone a holy light.
>
> African American spiritual, refrain; John W. Work Jr., 1872-1925, stanzas, alt.

CHRISTMAS 1: PROMISE FULFILLED

Mantra Prayer

O God, I don't know where to start.
Come make a stable in my heart.
In times of darkness, pain, and fear,
Lord, meet me here. Lord, meet me here.

Scripture: Luke 2:1, 3-14

In those days a decree went out from Emperor Augustus that all the world should be registered.... All went to their own towns to be registered. Joseph also went from the town of Nazareth in Galilee to Judea, to the city of David called Bethlehem, because he was descended from the house and family of David. He went to be registered with Mary, to whom he was engaged and who was expecting a child. While they were there, the time came for her to deliver her child. And she gave birth to her firstborn son and wrapped him in bands of cloth, and laid him in a manger, because there was no place for them in the inn. In that region there were shepherds living in the fields, keeping watch over their flock by night. Then an angel of the Lord stood before them, and the glory of the Lord shone around them, and they were terrified. But the angel said to them, "Do not be afraid; for see—I am bringing you good news of great joy for all the people: to you is born this day in the city of David a Savior, who is the Messiah, the Lord. This will be a sign for you: you will find a child wrapped in bands of cloth and lying in a manger." And suddenly there was with the angel a multitude of the heavenly host, praising God and saying, "Glory to God in the highest heaven, and on earth peace among those whom he favors!"

Reflection

Our flawed human nature means that the word *promise* too often means "disappointment." Around us and in our own lives, promises have not been kept. Promises of presence, love, money, materials, time—all broken and replaced with anger, grief, and confusion. These moments of discord occur on many levels: promises between friends, vows among loved ones, agreements made by governments. It is easy to get caught up in the disappointment, overwhelmed by feelings of anger and distrust, or guilt and self-hatred. "God, where are you?" we cry out, joining the cries of centuries of people yearning for a relationship that is whole and holy. Whom can we trust?

The Christmas story is the fulfillment of a promise. God says, "I will be with you." Through the birth of Jesus, God comes to earth, bringing light and life to all people. The setting God chooses for this story is striking. Jesus is not born into wealth and power. Instead, he is born to a young couple, Mary and Joseph, in a stable for animals. Into this poverty, a Savior is born. This is not just the birth of a baby. It is the birth of peace. The birth of hope. It is the birth of grace—God's unconditional love for all people. God's love for you.

For the past three years, I have directed a women's prison choir called the Voices of Hope. For the first Christmas, I wanted to give everyone a gift, but prison rules prohibited bringing anything in. So, I wrote them a song:

> When you've said your goodbyes to the ones that you love,
> And you're feeling alone and it's not enough,
> When you're stuck in your head and you lose control
> Of the battle of worth in your mind and soul . . .
>
> Sing a new song, sing a song of peace.
> For the song that you sing will set you free.
> Sing, sing a new song of hope—
> It will be with you always wherever you go.

God is the song in our hearts. We are often too busy or loud or anxious to hear it, but God continues to sing a new song in our lives. God is always with us, and this promise of presence is the best present of all.

A Quote to Ponder

If holiness and the awful power and majesty of God were present in this least auspicious of all events, this birth of a peasant's child, then there is no place or time so lowly and earthbound but that holiness can be present there too.

—Frederick Buechner[10]

A Question to Wonder About

Where do themes of trust and promise arise for you in prison?

Prayer

Sustaining God, you have promised to be with us in times of joy and sorrow, yet we confess that we do not always trust in your presence. Thank you for sending your Son, Jesus, to live among us, to heal and comfort us, and to preach a radical word of love and grace to the world. May we carry this song in our heart as a reminder of your steadfast promise. And may your loving faithfulness be reflected in our own thoughts and actions toward ourselves and one another. In Jesus' name we pray. Amen.

Song

Joy to the World

> Joy to the world, the Lord is come!
> Let earth receive her king;
> let ev'ry heart prepare him room
> and heav'n and nature sing,
> and heav'n and nature sing,
> and heav'n, and heav'n and nature sing.
>
> Isaac Watts, 1674-1748

CHRISTMAS 2: GRACE UPON GRACE

Mantra Prayer
God who is greater than all time and space,
help me say YES! to receiving your grace.

Scripture: John 1:1-5, 14, 16
In the beginning was the Word, and the Word was with God, and the Word was God. He was in the beginning with God. All things came into being through him, and without him not one thing came into being. What has come into being in him was life, and the life was the light of all people. The light shines in the darkness, and the darkness did not overcome it. . . . And the Word became flesh and lived among us, and we have seen his glory, the glory as of a father's only son, full of grace and truth. . . . From his fullness we have all received, grace upon grace.

Reflection
Although *grace* is not a word we use much in our day-to-day living, it is one of the core concepts of Christian belief. Grace is God's love freely given to us, with no strings attached. There is nothing we can do that can win God's love. Similarly, none of our failings will keep God from loving us. This can be a difficult concept to understand, since our human relationships don't usually work like this. We are used to gaining trust, building friendships, and growing to love others. We have pushed others away or been pushed away when we have made hurtful choices. Yet God, who created us and knows every aspect of our being, has loved us and will continue to love us unconditionally. It can be hard to accept God's grace. We feel undeserving: Why would anyone love me?

At the first Voices of Hope prison choir rehearsal, the walls of that prison had never heard such beautiful music. I looked out at a room full of eager singers rediscovering hope and joy in the music. That is, all except for one woman who was sobbing in the back row. The rehearsal went on for an hour, and she cried the entire time. Just before the end, I asked her if everything was OK. "I don't know what's happening to me," she exclaimed. "I never cry!"

How often do we come at the world with our arms up, ready to fight? We build walls and resist all feeling. When we do this, we are not just protecting ourselves from bad things; we are refusing the good as well. But God is already there at work in us. We do not have to earn God's grace. We just receive it as a gift.

A Quote to Ponder
God's grace is a gift that is freely given to us. We don't earn a thing when it comes to God's love, and we only try to live in response to the gift.... We can't, through our piety or goodness, move closer to God. God is always coming near to us.
—Nadia Bolz-Weber[11]

A Question to Wonder About
How might you be standing in your own way of receiving God's grace in the form of Jesus Christ?

Prayer
God of grace, you love us as your own. When we want to keep out the good you have for us, make a way into our hearts. When we feel broken, mend us. When we doubt your grace, assure us that your song is true and lovely, even when we sing through our tears. I ask this in Jesus' name. Amen.

Song
Amazing Grace, How Sweet the Sound

> Amazing grace! how sweet the sound
> that saved a wretch like me!
> I once was lost, but now am found;
> was blind, but now I see.
>
> John Newton, 1725-1807, alt.

BRIGHT STAR RISING: EPIPHANY

Mantra Prayer
Lord Jesus, I have traveled far
in search of you—the brightest star.
Adjusted to the dark of night,
may I take comfort in your light.

Scripture: Matthew 2:1-2
In the time of King Herod, after Jesus was born in Bethlehem
of Judea, wise men from the East came to Jerusalem, asking,
"Where is the child who has been born king of the Jews?
For we observed his star at its rising, and have come to pay
him homage."

Reflection
Epiphany is the season of light. High in the night sky, above
the stable where Jesus is born, a star shines brightly. This star
is a literal illumination that draws the world to God's love,
which has come to earth as a newborn baby. Epiphany is also
a light within our own hearts. In this season, we come to know
the radical ministry of Jesus and our call to travel by the light
that is Jesus. And we are never the same again.

Jesus is not your ordinary teacher. His subversive message turns social order on its head, instructing his students to love their enemies and lift up the poor and lowly. Even more surprising is that Jesus isn't just *preaching* radical hospitality—he's *practicing* it. Jesus' ministry transforms pain and sorrow into blessing. Jesus spends his time at the edges of society, where his followers witness him performing miracles: turning water into wine at the wedding in Cana, healing the sick, and casting out demons.

As we get to know these stories, we too become followers of Jesus. God has shown up and will continue to show up in our lives at unexpected times and in unexpected ways, ready to mold us into the best version of ourselves. When we pray, when we build community, when we journey over mountains and through valleys, we are changed. Together let us sing: "This little light of mine, I'm gonna let it shine!"

A Quote to Ponder
We were born to make manifest the glory of God that is within us. It's not just in some of us; it's in everyone. And as we let our own light shine, we unconsciously give other people permission to do the same. As we are liberated from our own fear, our presence automatically liberates others. —Marianne Williamson[12]

A Question to Wonder About
What is one way that you might let your light shine?

Song
This Little Light of Mine

> This little light of mine, I'm goin'-a let it shine; (3x)
> let it shine, let it shine, let it shine.
> African American spiritual

Light Dawns on a Weary World

What has come into being in him was life, and the life was the light of all people.

—John 1:3-4

TIME AFTER EPIPHANY 1: JOURNEY TOWARD JUSTICE

Mantra Prayer

Light out of darkness
Comfort from despair
Peace fueled by justice
Lord, hear my prayer.

Scripture: Matthew 2:7-12, 16

Then Herod secretly called for the wise men and learned from them the exact time when the star had appeared. Then he sent them to Bethlehem, saying, "Go and search diligently for the child; and when you have found him, bring me word so that I may also go and pay him homage." When they had heard the king, they set out; and there, ahead of them, went the star that they had seen at its rising, until it stopped over the place where the child was. When they saw that the star had stopped, they were overwhelmed with joy. On entering the house, they saw the child with Mary his mother; and they knelt down and paid him homage. Then, opening their treasure chests, they offered him gifts of gold, frankincense, and myrrh. And having been warned in a dream not to return to Herod, they left for their own country by another road. . . . When Herod saw that he had been tricked by the wise men, he was infuriated, and he sent and killed all the children in and around Bethlehem who were two years old or under, according to the time that he had learned from the wise men.

Reflection

Often when we tell the Christmas story, we emphasize the joy of Jesus' birth. People near and far were drawn to the light; three wise men traveled quite a distance to bring gifts to the newborn king. But not everyone was happy. King Herod was afraid. The birth of Jesus was a direct threat to his power, so King Herod ordered that all children in Bethlehem age two and under be killed. The irony is that Jesus was never in competition with King Herod.

Lana joined the Voices of Hope women's prison choir in our first quarter and quickly showed her commitment to singing. She became a leader in the choir, and was making big strides as well toward earning her GED diploma. Suddenly, she was gone. The other singers explained that she had been transferred overnight to another facility. Transfers at a moment's notice were frequent. Lana's efforts to make positive change were not rewarded. Where is the justice in this system?

Through Jesus' ministry, God introduces a new and radical vision of justice: an inclusive community, a "kin-dom" built out of mutuality, respect, and love for one another. Jesus gives us a vision of a world where the poor will be lifted up, those imprisoned will be released, the sick will be healed, and all who are oppressed will be freed from their burdens.

Not everyone likes what Jesus has to say, and his disciples find that following Jesus is no easy task. We inevitably face Herods along our way. Are you ready for the journey?

A Quote to Ponder
I have walked that long road to freedom. I have tried not to falter; I have made missteps along the way. . . . I have taken a moment here to rest, to steal a view of the glorious vista that surrounds me, to look back on the distance I have come. But I can rest only for a moment, for with freedom come responsibilities, and I dare not linger, for my long walk is not yet ended. —Nelson Mandela[13]

A Question to Wonder About
Who are the Herods that you face on your journey?

Prayer
Saving God, we are on a long journey and we need your direction. It is not just these prison walls that are keeping us bound. It's the way we think and feel about ourselves. It's the walls we have built up between one another. It's our attempts to hide from you. Make yourself known in this place, O God. May we accept the call of the prophets who have gone before us, that we serve you with love and peace. In Jesus' name. Amen.

Song
Guide My Feet

> Guide my feet while I run this race.
> Guide my feet while I run this race.
> Guide my feet while I run this race.
> for I don't want to run this race in vain.
>
> Hold my hand . . .
> Stand by me . . .
> I'm your child . . .
> Search my heart . . .
> African American spiritual

TIME AFTER EPIPHANY 2: CALLED BY NAME

Mantra Prayer
I am a child of God.

*Each time you touch water, repeat this mantra. You may
even like to dip your finger in water and draw a cross
on your forehead or the palm of your hand. This symbol
marks you as God's own; you are loved and sealed with the
cross of Christ forever.*

Scriptures: Luke 3:15-16
As the people were filled with expectation, and all were
questioning in their hearts concerning John, whether he
might be the Messiah, John answered all of them by saying, "I
baptize you with water; but one who is more powerful than I is
coming; I am not worthy to untie the thong of his sandals. He
will baptize you with the Holy Spirit and fire."

Isaiah 43:1
But now thus says the LORD, he who created you, O Jacob, he
who formed you, O Israel: Do not fear, for I have redeemed you;
I have called you by name, you are mine.

Reflection
I have learned from the Voices of Hope women's prison choir
how important it is to be called by name. This lesson came
to life on what seemed like a very ordinary day of choir. We
had been doing some basic songwriting, and we invited some
guests into the prison for a performance. Since the guest
musicians made it through security with time to spare, we
quickly wrote a song for the women in the choir. We decided
that we would sing the words "We listen to the Voices of
Hope," followed by each singer's name: "We listen to Vanessa,

we listen to Angelique . . ."—about twenty-five women in all. It seemed like a simple idea, and we were not prepared for the impact.

When it came time to share the song, we started through the list of names. The first few were shocked. "Hey, that's me!" someone said, smiling. As they caught on to the pattern, everyone fell silent. You could see women waiting to hear their name, and one by one, as each person's name was called, tears streamed down her face.

God calls each of us by name. In baptism we are marked with the cross of Christ, a sign that God has sacrificed everything to say, "I love you." No matter who we are or what path led us to this moment, the waters of baptism wash us clean, affirming our belonging in God's holy family. Your name is not offender, inmate, felon, or prisoner. You are not a number or a forgotten identity. Your name is "Beloved Child of God."

A Quote to Ponder

We all experience sadness, we all come at times to despair, and we all lose hope that the suffering in our lives and in our world will ever end. I want to share with you my faith and my understanding that this suffering can be transformed and redeemed. There is no such thing as a totally hopeless case. . . . God is transforming the world now—through us—because God loves us. —Desmond Tutu[14]

A Question to Wonder About

What does your full name mean to you?

Prayer

O God of new life, you moved over the waters of creation, and out of chaos, you brought forth beauty. We confess that at times, we have continued to perpetuate paths of destruction and despair. Let your baptismal grace wash over us, that we may be given new life. Claim us as your own, and be with us on our journey as your children. In Jesus' name. Amen.

Song
I Am Becoming

> I am not the person I used to be,
> I am not the person I want to be,
> but I am becoming.
> I am not the future, I am not the past,
> all I have is now within my grasp,
> but I am becoming . . .
> I am becoming home to myself.
>
> Linda Kachelmeier[15]

FREE US FROM OUR PAST: LENT

ASH WEDNESDAY: DUST BREATHED INTO LIFE

Mantra Prayer
Walk with me on my journey, and point me to you.

Scripture: Psalm 51:10-12
Create in me a clean heart, O God,
    and renew a right spirit within me.
Cast me not away from your presence,
    and take not your Holy Spirit from me.
Restore to me the joy of your salvation
    and sustain me with your bountiful Spirit.

My God, My God, Why Have You Forsaken Me?

*O LORD, my God, my Savior, by
day and night I cry to you.*

—Psalm 88:1

Reflection

Ash Wednesday begins the forty-day spiritual journey of Lent, an opportunity to ponder things that keep us from trusting God fully. Acts of generosity, prayer, and fasting are the "disciplines of Lent." But time in prison is a forced fasting from much of what life used to be. And religious practices can be used, like much puffed-up prison behavior, like trophies to impress others. The forty days of Lent are exactly the opposite—a time to look inward.

As Lent begins on Ash Wednesday, it is common for a pastor or priest to smear the sign of the cross on a person's forehead with ashes and say, "Remember that you are dust, and to dust you shall return." This dusty sign of the cross reminds us that Jesus himself endured great suffering and understands all our pain. God goes with us into and through the harshest experiences of our lives.

In the world, we are often defined by how we succeed or fail. For those in prison, the stigma of failure clings close, like a demon wanting to mark us as "flunked out," not only now but for the rest of life. The message repeats daily: "Offender, criminal, felon . . ." But God's message on this day of ash and dust is that we are not known by our faults or crimes, our mistakes or wrong choices.

We are created from dust and will return to dust (Genesis 3:19). Those bold words make us face the reality of death. And we face many kinds of death: broken relationships, separations from loved ones, powerlessness in a punishing world, rejection, ruined reputation, lost job, lost home, lost money, lost family, lost health, lost desire—all the broken pieces of our lives. But those words also tell us about God's power to create something new. From what is trampled on and swept away as dirt, God creates life and says, "It is good" (Genesis 1).

Whatever your DOC number, offender status, or sentence from the state, you will not be cast away from God's presence. You will not be denied the hope and joy of salvation.

A Quote to Ponder
And so let this be
a season for wandering,
for trusting the breaking,
for tracing the rupture
that will return you

to the One who waits,
who watches,
who works within
the rending
to make your heart

whole.
—Jan Richardson[16]

A Question to Wonder About
How might God be repairing what feels broken in your life?

Prayer
Holy God, who journeys with us in all the places of our lives: Be with us throughout this season. Open our hearts to know and speak truth in our lives and to see you as our way and our life. Guide us to trust that you are working to make all things new and whole. In Jesus' name we pray. Amen.

Song
I Want Jesus to Walk with Me

> I want Jesus to walk with me;
> I want Jesus to walk with me;
> all along my pilgrim journey,
> Lord, I want Jesus to walk with me.
>
> In my trials, Lord, walk with me;
> in my trials, Lord, walk with me;
> when my heart is almost breaking,
> Lord, I want Jesus to walk with me.

African American spiritual

LENT 1: PAINFUL TRUTH

Mantra Prayer
Turn me to you, God, and free me from my past.

Scripture: Ephesians 2:1-10
You were dead through the trespasses and sins in which you once lived, following the course of this world, following the ruler of the power of the air, the spirit that is now at work among those who are disobedient. All of us once lived among them in the passions of our flesh, following the desires of flesh and senses, and we were by nature children of wrath, like everyone else. But God, who is rich in mercy, out of the great love with which he loved us even when we were dead through our trespasses, made us alive together with Christ—by grace you have been saved—and raised us up with him and seated us with him in the heavenly places in Christ Jesus, so that in the ages to come he might show the immeasurable riches of his grace in kindness toward us in Christ Jesus. For by grace you

have been saved through faith, and this is not your own doing; it is the gift of God—not the result of works, so that no one may boast. For we are what he has made us, created in Christ Jesus for good works, which God prepared beforehand to be our way of life.

Reflection

Naming our regrets. Naming things we have done or not done that have caused harm. Naming the ways our lives have gone wrong. All of this is repentance. Demeaning, manipulating, or shaming other people is not repentance. Seeking the way toward God is repentance. The word *repent* means "to turn around," to go back, to change direction from ways that are destructive and move in the direction of God's love.

One thing that happens frequently and in its own peculiar way in prison is the naming of guilt in others rather than being honest about our own guilt. Assigning a hierarchy of crimes. Detailing offenses. Blaming snitches or cops or informers, unfair judges, bad laws, and ineffective lawyers. These are all ways we avoid facing our own sin and guilt. But that blame only makes us prisoners of the past and keeps us locked away from the gift of a greater, forgiven life. That life is what God intends for us, and repentance frees us to discover it.

To repent does not mean agreeing to a plea deal. It's not a threat: "Repent or else!" And it does not mean that punishment for wrongdoing will disappear. Repentance opens the way to heal broken relationships with other people, with communities, and with God. Repentance is the way to set yourself free.

A Quote to Ponder

Honesty is often very hard. The truth is often painful. But the freedom it can bring is worth the trying. —Fred Rogers[17]

A Question to Wonder About

What freedom does it give you to name your regrets truthfully, even when it's painful?

Prayer

Merciful God, who rescues us through the free gift of love in Jesus Christ: Turn us from our failings toward you. Give us faith to know your grace and trust that you forgive us for all the ways we mess up. Inspire us to seek you out and to live in ways that lead to full, rich, joy-filled lives. In the name of Jesus we pray. Amen.

Song

Give Me Jesus

> In the morning when I rise, in the morning when I rise,
> in the morning when I rise, give me Jesus.
>
> Give me Jesus, give me Jesus.
> You may have all the rest, give me Jesus.
>
> African American spiritual

LENT 2: GUIDANCE ALONG THE JOURNEY

Mantra Prayer

Jesus, guide me; tempter, depart!

Scripture: Luke 4:1-13

Jesus, full of the Holy Spirit, returned from the Jordan and was led by the Spirit in the wilderness, where for forty days he was tempted by the devil. He ate nothing at all during those days, and when they were over, he was famished. The devil said to him, "If you are the Son of God, command this stone to become a loaf of bread." Jesus answered him, "It is written, 'One does not live by bread alone.'" Then the devil led him up and showed him in an instant all the kingdoms of the world. And the devil said to him, "To you I will give their glory and all this authority; for it has been given over to me, and I give it to anyone I please. If you, then, will worship me, it will all be yours." Jesus answered him, "It is written, 'Worship the Lord your God, and serve only him.'" Then the devil took him to Jerusalem, and placed him on the pinnacle of the temple, saying to him, "If you are the Son of God, throw yourself down from here, for it is written, 'He will command his angels concerning you, to protect you,' and 'On their hands they will bear you up, so that you will not dash your foot against a stone.'" Jesus answered him, "It is said, 'Do not put the Lord your God to the test.'" When the devil had finished every test, he departed from him until an opportune time.

Reflection

If you think about it, the temptation of Jesus is a story about what comes at us every day. Jesus was tempted to turn stone into bread. He'd been fasting for forty days. If you're desperately hungry, have seemingly nothing, or want something so badly, that can become the fateful reason for doing whatever it takes to get what you need.

Jesus was tempted to believe that all the kingdoms of the world—kingdoms the devil claimed for himself—held all the pleasure and meaning in life. If you feel unimportant or cheated by life, or desperate for happiness or power, that can become the fateful reason for doing whatever it takes to get respect.

Jesus was tempted to hurl himself down from a high pinnacle to prove that God would protect him. If there is danger on the street or around the corner, if there are threats or insults, then proving you're not afraid and that you're too strong to be hurt can become the fateful reason for doing whatever it takes to protect yourself.

The temptations that lead to prison also follow you right through the gates. They don't go away. Notice the last sentence in the scripture reading that says the devil wasn't done with Jesus: "He departed from him until an opportune time."

Jesus exposed the devil as a con—a tempter offering nothing but a bad ending. But the struggles go on. And because you and I are not Jesus, sometimes temptations get the better of us and we fall for the con job. The point of the story—the gift of these forty days in the wilderness of Lent—is to find encouragement from Jesus, who has been there, and will go back there to be with us whenever the con artist shows up again.

A Quote to Ponder
Each of us is more than the worst thing we've ever done.
—Bryan Stevenson[18]

A Question to Wonder About
What temptations are you currently facing, and how can Jesus help you overcome them?

Prayer
Sustaining God, who shelters us in our time of storm: Open our eyes to the presence of the Holy Spirit in our midst. Give us strength when the temptations of our lives seem too great. And remind us that you are the victor over sin, death, and the devil. In Jesus' name we pray. Amen.

Song
Jesus Is a Rock in a Weary Land

> Jesus is a rock in a weary land,
> a weary land, a weary land;
> my Jesus is a rock in a weary land,
> a shelter in the time of storm.
>
> Yonder comes my Savior,
> him whom I love so well;
> he has the palm of victory
> and the keys of death and hell.
> African American spiritual

LENT 3: SOMETHING MADE NEW

Mantra Prayer
God, you have the power to make a way out of no way.

Scriptures: Isaiah 43:18-19
Do not remember the former things, or consider the things of old. I am about to do a new thing; now it springs forth, do you not perceive it? I will make a way in the wilderness and rivers in the desert.

2 Corinthians 5:17-18

So if anyone is in Christ, there is a new creation: everything old has passed away; see, everything has become new! All this is from God....

Reflection

Many conversations inside the fences of a prison start this way: "Where will you be and what will you do when you get out?" The answers are divided between an obsession "not to go back to ..." and a determination "to return to ...." If you pay attention, the talk is all about believing there is something there, or nothing there; someone there, or no one there; good fortune there, or trouble there. But missing from most of the conversations, like a washed-out bridge on the road to somewhere, is an awareness that not everything about life depends on where it is lived—not even whether inside or outside of prison.

Another conversation going around in prison starts like this: "After you get arrested and go to prison, you find out who your friends are and who are not." True enough. For many, it feels like another bridge washed out.

Into both the uneasiness and the hopefulness about where life will take shape and with whom it will be lived, into uncertainties about the past or about the future, comes God's message from a prophet, Isaiah, and an apostle, Paul. The message is this: "I'm doing a new thing."

Often it feels like once something is broken, it will forever be that way for us. But if you dare to let God join the conversation, listen and hear this: In every hard thing, in suffering and even in death, you have reason to hope for new life. Hope happens in places we can't imagine, among people who will surprise us, in times we don't expect, and in ways we could never plan. This is the power of Jesus and the work of the Spirit to make all things new.

A Quote to Ponder

There's a part of all of us that longs to know that even what's weakest about us is still redeemable and can ultimately count for something good. —Fred Rogers[19]

A Question to Wonder About

Can you catch a glimpse of how God is making things new in your own situation?

Prayer

Merciful God, help us to have faith that you are able to make all things new. Restore us to you when things are difficult, uncertain, or broken. Give us hope and help us find a way when there seems to be no way; through Jesus Christ our Lord. Amen.

Song

I Heard the Voice of Jesus Say

> I heard the voice of Jesus say,
> "Come unto me and rest;
> lay down, O weary one, lay down
> your head upon my breast."
> I came to Jesus as I was,
> so weary, worn, and sad;
> I found in him a resting-place,
> and he has made me glad.
> Horatius Bonar, 1808-1889

PALM/PASSION SUNDAY: A FOOL'S PARADE?

Mantra Prayer
Blessed is the one who comes in the name of the Lord! Hosanna!

Scripture: Mark 11:1-10
When they were approaching Jerusalem, at Bethphage and Bethany, near the Mount of Olives, he sent two of his disciples and said to them, "Go into the village ahead of you, and immediately as you enter it, you will find tied there a colt that has never been ridden; untie it and bring it. If anyone says to you, 'Why are you doing this?' just say this, 'The Lord needs it and will send it back here immediately.'" They went away and found a colt tied near a door, outside in the street. As they were untying it, some of the bystanders said to them, "What are you doing, untying the colt?" They told them what Jesus had said; and they allowed them to take it. Then they brought the colt to Jesus and threw their cloaks on it; and he sat on it. Many people spread their cloaks on the road, and others spread leafy branches that they had cut in the fields. Then those who went ahead and those who followed were shouting, "Hosanna! Blessed is the one who comes in the name of the Lord! Blessed is the coming kingdom of our ancestor David! Hosanna in the highest heaven!"

Reflection
Jesus' triumphant entry into Jerusalem starts as a parade like many parades. A leader enters a city, and followers sing and shout praises. However, in this story, that leader is a poor religious teacher riding a donkey, and his followers are the outcasts and the powerless of society. The event begins as a celebration but soon seems nothing more than a fool's parade. When the authorities get involved, Jesus—the hero of the cheering crowd—is betrayed by one friend, and another denies

ever knowing him. Arrested. Tried. Sentenced. Executed. So much for hope!

But a major miscalculation was made by most who counted on Jesus to change the circumstances of their miserable lives— which, under Roman power, were indeed miserable. They were all about cheering for a fighter. Understandable. It's what they knew in a violent and unjust world. So Jesus was more than a disappointment; he seemed both fool and failure. Most of the people in the crowd were content to see him die.

Still, the people's disillusionment, his friends' betrayals, and the authorities' edicts would not and could not determine how Jesus would lead. He would choose the weak above the strong, the least to be greatest, the last to be first. He would choose mercy over vengeance, love instead of hate. And for that, he would die.

But Palm Sunday is only the beginning event. The fool's parade moves toward peace and justice. Holy Week begins here, with more questions than answers. How do you promote peace and do justice? In a world where the least go unnoticed, the poor are ignored, people are imprisoned unjustly, and multitudes remain hungry and homeless, how do you respond?

As Holy Week unfolds, Jesus shows a way.

A Quote to Ponder
This week invites us to consider how we are moving through our own journey—through Lent as well as through life. Are we allowing ourselves to be swept along by circumstances, traveling our road by default? Or are we seeking to walk with intention and discernment, creating our path with some measure of the courage and clarity by which Christ walked

his, even in the midst of forces that may lie beyond our control? —Jan Richardson[20]

A Question to Wonder About

What are some ways that you might promote peace and justice in your life and relationships, even while in prison?

Prayer

Triumphant God, who enters into our lives as Jesus entered Jerusalem on a donkey: Guide us so that our worship may be focused on you and our lives might seek the eternal peace and justice you desire. As we hear the story of Jesus' betrayal, trial, and death, guide us to draw closer to you and to live in ways that bring about peace and justice in the world. In Jesus' name we pray. Amen.

Song

We Are Marching in the Light (*Siyahamba*)

> We are marching in the light of God,
> we are marching in the light of God.
> We are marching in the light of God,
> we are marching in the light of God.
>
> We are marching, marching, we are marching, marching,
> we are marching in the light of God.
> We are marching, marching, we are marching, marching,
> we are marching in the light of God.
>
> We are dancing ...
> We are praying ...
> We are singing ...
> South African traditional[21]

MAUNDY THURSDAY: THE CHALLENGE OF LOVE

Mantra Prayer
Breathe in the assurance of God's promise.
  (*Inhale God's promise.*)
Breathe out a commitment to spread God's love.
  (*Exhale God's love.*)

Scripture: John 13:3-10, 12-15, 34
[During supper,] Jesus, knowing that the Father had given all things into his hands, and that he had come from God and was going to God, got up from the table, took off his outer robe, and tied a towel around himself. Then he poured water into a basin and began to wash the disciples' feet and to wipe them with the towel that was tied around him. He came to Simon Peter, who said to him, "Lord, are you going to wash my feet?" Jesus answered, "You do not know now what I am doing, but later you will understand." Peter said to him, "You will never wash my feet." Jesus answered, "Unless I wash you, you have no share with me." Simon Peter said to him, "Lord, not my feet only but also my hands and my head!" Jesus said to him, "One who has bathed does not need to wash, except for the feet, but is entirely clean. And you are clean, though not all of you." . . . After he had washed their feet, had put on his robe, and had returned to the table, he said to them, "Do you know what I have done to you? You call me Teacher and Lord—and you are right, for that is what I am. So if I, your Lord and Teacher, have washed your feet, you also ought to wash one another's feet. For I have set you an example, that you also should do as I have done to you. . . . I give you a new commandment, that you love one another. Just as I have loved you, you also should love one another."

Reflection

One of the last things Jesus did with his disciples the night he was arrested was to wash their feet. It is one of the last memories his friends will have of being with him. For many of them, that act of foot-washing made no sense. It was a job for a servant, not a teacher. They were shocked—offended probably—that he would literally stoop so low. It was shameful. But with his hands on their dirty feet, Jesus teaches a new thing, showing love without limits. He gives a new command to love one another as he has loved them. Love stoops to a posture of humility and bends into acts of service.

Prison is a place where humiliation is a daily routine and where life is lived among people difficult to like and hard to love. This command of Jesus to love as he loves is an immense challenge, but no less a command.

Remarkably, Jesus loves without exception. Even knowing what it will cost him. Even knowing that among those to whom he stoops in service—those whose feet he will wash—are the ones whose feet will carry them as they run away from him. His love for us is that remarkable.

A Quote to Ponder

We have just religion enough to make us hate, but not enough to make us love one another. —Jonathan Swift[22]

A Question to Wonder About

How can you live out Jesus' immense challenge to love others, even in prison?

Prayer

Loving God, who shows us that true love is expressed through service: Move in us the will to love and serve others, even in the difficult places of our lives. When we feel alone, may we know your constant love. Open our eyes to see the needs of those around us and to show your love to all in need. In Jesus' name we pray. Amen.

Song
Great God, Your Love Has Called Us

> Great God, in Christ you call our name
> and then receive us as your own,
> not through some merit, right, or claim,
> but by your gracious love alone.
> We strain to glimpse your mercy seat
> and find you kneeling at our feet.
> Brian A. Wren, b. 1936[23]

GOOD FRIDAY: IT'S ALL THE GOOD NEWS WE GET

Mantra Prayer
God, give me hope, give me strength, give me Jesus.

Scripture: Matthew 27:1-2, 11-14, 22-23, 26, 33-38, 46, 50
When morning came, all the chief priests and the elders of the people conferred together against Jesus in order to bring about his death. They bound him, led him away, and handed him over to Pilate the governor. Now Jesus stood before the governor; and the governor asked him, "Are you the King of the Jews?" Jesus said, "You say so." But when he was accused by the chief priests and elders, he did not answer. Then Pilate said to him, "Do you not hear how many accusations they make against you?" But he gave him no answer, not even to a single charge, so that the governor was greatly amazed.... Pilate said

to [the crowd], "... What should I do with Jesus who is called the Messiah?" All of them said, "Let him be crucified!" Then he asked, "Why, what evil has he done?" But they shouted all the more, "Let him be crucified!" ... So ... after flogging Jesus, he handed him over to be crucified.... And when they came to a place called Golgotha (which means Place of a Skull), they offered him wine to drink, mixed with gall; but when he tasted it, he would not drink it. And when they had crucified him, they divided his clothes among themselves by casting lots; then they sat down there and kept watch over him. Over his head they put the charge against him, which read, "This is Jesus, the King of the Jews." Then two bandits were crucified with him, one on his right and one on his left.... And about three o'clock Jesus cried with a loud voice, "... My God, my God, why have you forsaken me?" ... Then Jesus cried again with a loud voice and breathed his last.

Reflection

On Good Friday we read the story of Jesus' trial, crucifixion, and death. We hear the questions asked of Jesus by his judge, Pilate. We hear how the crowd turned on Jesus after his parade into Jerusalem on Palm Sunday. The pain of his suffering and the violence of his death are remembered with gruesome detail. When Jesus cries out, "My God, my God, why have you forsaken me?" we hear words that could well be our own. They are echoes from so many chapters of our own lives cried in anger or mumbled in lonely silence from a prison cell.

But despite all its sadness and suffering, this story holds a glimpse of hope. We might struggle to grasp it, but this glimmer of hope comes down from the agony of the cross, where Jesus cries out to God with faith—even in the midst of torture, despair, and pain. On this Good Friday, that is all the good news that we get. But surprisingly, it will turn out to be good news indeed.

A Quote to Ponder
The reality of grief is the absence of God—"My God, my God, why hast thou forsaken me?" The reality of grief is the solitude of pain, the feeling that your heart is in pieces, your mind's a blank.... "My God, my God, why hast thou forsaken me?" Yes, but at least, "My God, my God." —William Sloane Coffin[24]

A Question to Wonder About
When you feel forsaken by God, can you still say, "*My* God"?

Prayer
Holy God, who suffered as Jesus Christ on the cross: Remain with us through all the suffering in our lives. Comfort us when we feel forsaken, when we fear judgment, when we confront betrayal, and when we face death. Give us the glimpse of hope and the assurance of your presence that we so desperately need. In Jesus' name we pray. Amen.

Song
Were You There

> Were you there when they crucified my Lord?
> Were you there when they crucified my Lord?
> Oh, sometimes it causes me to tremble, tremble, tremble.
> Were you there when they crucified my Lord?
>
> Were you there when they nailed him to the tree?...
> Were you there when they laid him in the tomb?...
> African American spiritual

HOLY SATURDAY: HOLDING ON

Mantra Prayer
I'm waiting to see how the story ends; I'm holding on.

Scripture: Matthew 27:57-61
When it was evening, there came a rich man from Arimathea, named Joseph, who was also a disciple of Jesus. He went to Pilate and asked for the body of Jesus; then Pilate ordered it to be given to him. So Joseph took the body and wrapped it in a clean linen cloth and laid it in his own new tomb, which he had hewn in the rock. He then rolled a great stone to the door of the tomb and went away. Mary Magdalene and the other Mary were there, sitting opposite the tomb.

Reflection
Holy Saturday is the one full day in the church year when Jesus is dead. It is a strange day for followers of Jesus who hoped their future included him with them. It is the kind of weird that is numbness after the worst news is announced or when the hardest suffering is endured. It's the weird numbness that settles in after the sentence is delivered, the punishment meted out. It is the hollowed-out emptiness that begins before and lasts longer than our tears.

There was no way for Jesus' followers to know what was coming; they had more to fear than they had to hope for. Possibilities of the future vanished into a space open only to grief and regret. Now what? Locked into numbness, they had nothing to do but wait. In prison, we wait too, doing time until the night of numbness awakens to what we cannot yet see but only dare to hope for.

A man now serving time, after he was arrested but before being sentenced, in that awful stretch of waiting for the judge's decision—a man who believed that everything he loved in his life had been destroyed—was asked by his counselor: "Why don't you kill yourself?" He answered, "Because I want to be around to see how this story ends."

In the waiting, we hold on. The story is not yet finished.

A Quote to Ponder
In you, O LORD, have I taken refuge; let me never be put to shame; deliver me in your righteousness. —Psalm 31:1

A Question to Wonder About
How do you hold on in the weird, numb waiting times?

Prayer
Jesus, you died as we will die. Be with us in our waiting. Help us to trust that we can hope in you, even in our hollowed-out emptiness when the way forward is unclear. In Jesus' name we pray. Amen.

Song
Stay with Me

> Stay with me, remain here with me.
> Watch and pray. Watch and pray.
> —Taizé Community[25]

In Death, There Is Yet Life

You have been born anew . . .
through the living and
enduring word of God.

—1 Peter 1:23

DYING TO LIVE A NEW LIFE: EASTER

Mantra Prayer
Christ is risen! The Lord is risen indeed! Alleluia!

Scripture: Luke 24:44-49
Then [Jesus] said to them, "These are my words that I spoke to you while I was still with you—that everything written about me in the law of Moses, the prophets, and the psalms must be fulfilled." Then he opened their minds to understand the scriptures, and he said to them, "Thus it is written, that the Messiah is to suffer and to rise from the dead on the third day, and that repentance and forgiveness of sins is to be proclaimed in his name to all nations, beginning from Jerusalem. You are witnesses of these things. And see, I am sending upon you what my Father promised; so stay here in the city until you have been clothed with power from on high."

Reflection
Easter Sunday is one of the most important and joy-filled days in the life of Christians. On Easter and for the fifty days following, Christians celebrate Jesus' victory over death and over the unjust powers that sent him to the cross to die. Easter is the fulfillment of Jesus' promise to reveal God's love to the world—a love that is greater than death and greater than any of the world's systems or leaders. In his death and resurrection, Jesus shows us God's faithfulness and presence with us, now and forever.

While our culture understands Easter as a time to color eggs and fill baskets with candy, Christians understand Easter as a time of new life, hope, and healing. The story of the resurrection reminds us that in death there is still life, like a new bud on a tree that can only break through when the leaf that was there before dies and falls away. We are called to this kind of life in Christ. We are called, particularly during Easter, to let die those things that prevent new life from springing forth in us.

We are all held captive by the world's systems, and God comes to set us free. Jesus' death and resurrection affirm for us that there is always time for God's love to break in. No one is beyond God's reach or beyond God's love.

Jesus said, "I am the resurrection and the life. Those who believe in me, even though they die, will live, and everyone who lives and believes in me will never die" (John 11:25-26). This is God's promise—not only eternal life, but life today, filled with God's grace, mercy, and love.

A Quote to Ponder
The resurrection is in part about the sheer toughness and persistence of God's love. When we have done our worst, God remains God—and remains committed to being our God.
—Rowan Williams[26]

A Question to Wonder About
How can you find hope, healing, and new life while living in a place built to punish and break you down?

Song
Now All the Vault of Heaven Resounds

> Oh, fill us, Lord, with dauntless love;
> set heart and will on things above
> that we conquer through your triumph;
> grant grace sufficient for life's day
> that by our lives we truly say:

"Christ has triumphed! He is living!"
Alleluia, alleluia, alleluia!

Paul Z. Strodach, 1876-1947, alt.

EASTER 1: A SEED BEGINS

Mantra Prayer
Loving God, plant in my heart the seed of new life.

Scripture: John 12:23-26
Jesus answered them, "The hour has come for the Son of Man to be glorified. Very truly, I tell you, unless a grain of wheat falls into the earth and dies, it remains just a single grain; but if it dies, it bears much fruit. Those who love their life lose it, and those who hate their life in this world will keep it for eternal life. Whoever serves me must follow me, and where I am, there will my servant be also. Whoever serves me, the Father will honor."

Reflection
In this passage of the Gospel of John, Jesus has arrived in Jerusalem with many of his followers. He knows that very soon he will be betrayed by one of them and turned over to the authorities. He will be given a sham trial, be beaten by the police, be found guilty of crimes he didn't commit, be convicted, and be put to death. He is trying to prepare his friends for all of this. They are hanging out together, and Jesus is trying to help them understand the cost of being associated with him and of carrying on after he is gone.

People from all over the area have heard about Jesus and how he has been healing and feeding people and mixing it up with local religious and political leaders. They like what they hear, but they don't know what it will mean for them to join him.

Jesus tells them about making sacrifices. He says that following him means giving up some things that get in the way of living as he calls them to live. He wants them to let go of their old way of life and their old way of thinking about what it means to be successful or powerful, because worldly things don't mean anything to God. He wants them to learn to let go—just like the little grain of wheat lets go of the tall stalk and falls to the ground and lands in rich soil. He wants them to trust that a life rooted in him will be filled with greater things than the world can provide..

Incarceration is all about letting go. Being incarcerated means letting go of freedom, family, and friends for a time—sometimes a very long time. It also means letting go of whatever it was that landed us here. And incarceration gives us an opportunity, if we choose to take it, to free ourselves of a way of life and a way of thinking that resulted in our being held captive. Jesus tells us that we were captive long before we were incarcerated, because we were held by our desires for power, money, violence, status, and the actions that fed these desires. He offers us a different way to live. Jesus encourages us to let these old ways die so that we can live more freely, even when we are not physically free.

A Quote to Ponder
Leaves don't drop, they just let go,
and make a place for seeds to grow.
Every season brings a change;
a seed is what a tree contains;
to die and live is life's refrain.
—Carrie Newcomer and Michael Maines[27]

A Question to Wonder About

What do you need to let go of or let die in yourself—old hurts, grudges, jealousies, anger, hopelessness—to make room for God's love to grow more fully within you?

Prayer

Gracious God, I know that in order to have life, parts of me that I have held onto for many years must die. Help me let go of the way of life that landed me in this place. Create in me a spirit, I pray, that welcomes all the possibilities of a new life rooted in Christ. Open my eyes to see Christ's love all around me, even behind these bars, and give me the courage to let things in my life that keep me from a closer relationship with you die. Grant me an open heart to plant seeds of hope and new life in this place. In Jesus' name. Amen.

Song

We Won't Leave Here Like We Came

> We won't leave here like we came, in Jesus' name.
> Bound, oppressed, afflicted, sick or lame.
> For the Spirit of the Lord is still the same.
> We won't leave here like we came, in Jesus' name.
> Maceo Woods[28]

EASTER 2: EMPTY TOMBS AND OPEN HEARTS

Mantra Prayer
Gracious God, fill me with the peace of knowing you are with me always.

Scripture: Matthew 28:1-10
After the sabbath, as the first day of the week was dawning, Mary Magdalene and the other Mary went to see the tomb. And suddenly there was a great earthquake; for an angel of the Lord, descending from heaven, came and rolled back the stone and sat on it. His appearance was like lightning, and his clothing white as snow. For fear of him the guards shook and became like dead men. But the angel said to the women, "Do not be afraid; I know that you are looking for Jesus who was crucified. He is not here; for he has been raised, as he said. Come, see the place where he lay. Then go quickly and tell his disciples, 'He has been raised from the dead, and indeed he is going ahead of you to Galilee; there you will see him.' This is my message for you." So they left the tomb quickly with fear and great joy, and ran to tell his disciples. Suddenly Jesus met them and said, "Greetings!" And they came to him, took hold of his feet, and worshiped him. Then Jesus said to them, "Do not be afraid; go and tell my brothers to go to Galilee; there they will see me."

Reflection
The two Marys in this story—"Mary Magdalene and the other Mary"—get to the tomb, and the body of Jesus is gone! They don't know what to think. They encounter an angel sitting on the stone that had closed the opening to the tomb, who tells them all is well, that Jesus was raised from the dead, and that he will meet them in Galilee. Up to this point, the Marys and all of Jesus' followers must have been reeling after seeing him executed by the Roman government.

Imagine how hopeless they must have felt. They had followed him for three years, watching him stand up to the oppressors in their communities and welcome everyone, regardless of their economic status, or where they were from, or what kind of work they did. He had loved and welcomed all of them, but now he was gone. He had told them he would return after three days, but did they really believe that would happen? This passage shows us their awe and joy at realizing that Jesus had kept his promise. He was still, and would always be, with them!

Being locked up, away from family, friends, and community, can leave us feeling alone and abandoned. Yet in these lonely and broken places, Jesus meets us. The tomb did not hold Jesus in, and the walls of this institution will not hold him out. He arrived here long before anyone else and will remain long after everyone goes home. Walk with him in these corridors, sit with him in these cells, and welcome the hope he offers for a life not bounded by death or steel doors, but by love that is greater than both.

A Quote to Ponder
The good news of the resurrection of Jesus is not that we shall die and go home to him, but that he has risen and comes home with us, bringing all his hungry, naked, thirsty, sick, prisoner brothers and sisters with him. —Clarence Jordan[29]

A Question to Wonder About
Where has Jesus surprised you with hope in your current circumstances, and how do you help others find hope in their lives?

Prayer
God of joy and surprises, fill my heart with hope because it is hard to be hopeful in a place like this. Let me not be afraid of

what lies ahead, but trust that you are always with me. Take away my anxieties and fear so I can see you more clearly and meet you where you wait for me. Guide me every day on the road that leads always to you. In Jesus' name. Amen.

Song
If You but Trust in God to Guide You

> If you but trust in God to guide you
> with gentle hand through all your ways,
> you'll find that God is there beside you
> when crosses come, in trying days.
> Trust then in God's unchanging love;
> build on the rock that will not move.
>
> The Lord our restless hearts is holding,
> in peace and quietness content.
> We rest in God's good will unfolding,
> what wisdom from on high has sent.
> God, who has chosen us by grace,
> knows very well the fears we face.
>
> Georg Neumark, 1621-1681

EASTER 3: NO DOUBT WE'RE ALL WOUNDED

Mantra Prayer
Heal me, hands of Jesus, and make me whole again.

Scripture: John 20:24-29
But Thomas (who was called the Twin), one of the twelve, was not with them when Jesus came. So the other disciples told him, "We have seen the Lord." But he said to them, "Unless I see the mark of the nails in his hands, and put my finger in the

mark of the nails and my hand in his side, I will not believe." A week later his disciples were again in the house, and Thomas was with them. Although the doors were shut, Jesus came and stood among them and said, "Peace be with you." Then he said to Thomas, "Put your finger here and see my hands. Reach out your hand and put it in my side. Do not doubt but believe." Thomas answered him, "My Lord and my God!" Jesus said to him, "Have you believed because you have seen me? Blessed are those who have not seen and yet have come to believe."

Reflection

When Jesus returned to his disciples after the resurrection, the wounds from the nails in his hands and feet and from the spear in his side were still open and visible. He carried the wounds from that experience with him, just as we carry the invisible wounds from our experiences with us. Thomas needed proof that Jesus was real. He needed to touch the wounds in order to believe that this was the same man he had seen dying on a cross just a few days earlier.

In this passage from John's gospel, we learn that even when God transforms our lives, it doesn't mean that everything from our old lives gets left behind. Jesus shows us that the healing process doesn't start until our wounds have been seen, felt, and acknowledged. It is Jesus who helps us heal our wounds, whatever they are.

Jesus invites Thomas—and us—to come to him with our doubts and fears, our hurts and heartbreaks, and to be healed by his love for us.

A Quote to Ponder

Healing begins where the wound was made. —Alice Walker[30]

A Question to Wonder About

What wounds are still open in your heart, mind, or soul, and how might you let Jesus in to heal them?

Prayer

God of love, give me the courage of Thomas to seek your presence in the wounds I still carry in my body, mind, and spirit. I have been hurt and harmed in my life, and I have hurt and harmed others. Grant me your mercy as I work to heal what has been broken in me, in my family, and in my community. As you came before your disciples with your wounds still open, I come before you now with the remnants of my past laid bare, seeking the healing power of your love and the promise of new life in you. In Jesus' name I pray. Amen.

Song

Heal Me, Hands of Jesus

> Heal me, hands of Jesus,
> and search out all my pain;
> restore my hope, remove my fear
> and bring me peace again.
>
> Cleanse me, blood of Jesus,
> take bitterness away;
> let me forgive as one forgiven
> and bring me peace today.
> Michael Perry[31]

EASTER 4: LIVING WITH THANKFULNESS

Mantra Prayer
Break my heart open in the breaking of the bread.

Scripture: Mark 14:22-24
While they were eating, [Jesus] took a loaf of bread, and after blessing it he broke it, gave it to them, and said, "Take; this is my body." Then he took a cup, and after giving thanks he gave it to them, and all of them drank from it. He said to them, "This is my blood of the covenant, which is poured out for many."

Reflection
On the night before Jesus was going to be executed, he ate his last meal with his friends. This is often called the "Last Supper." He broke bread and poured wine and shared it with all of them. He told them to do the same thing together after he was gone, in order to remember his life, death, and resurrection. Jesus knew that life would be hard for his friends after his death. He knew they would be disrespected, bullied, and even killed simply for believing in him. So, on this final night with them, he gave them himself in the form of bread and wine, assuring them that whenever they broke bread together in this way, his presence, grace, love, forgiveness, and mercy would be with them. This is true for us still today.

Every Sunday millions of Christians around the world gather in churches to share bread and wine around a table (or altar), just as Jesus' earliest followers did. This meal has different names in different traditions: Eucharist, Holy Communion, the Lord's Supper, Breaking the Bread. We give thanks for all the blessings in our lives. We pray for peace and healing in the church, the world, our communities, and our families.

We confess to God and one another the things we have done, and the things we have not done, that have caused harm to ourselves and others. We accept the bread and wine as a gift from our loving God: The gift of Jesus' presence with us now. An invitation into a transformed future.

Luke 24 tells how after Jesus' resurrection, he joined two travelers on the way to the village of Emmaus. Even though they knew Jesus well, they didn't recognize that he was the one with them on that road. After all, Jesus had just been executed and buried! But when evening came, they saw him break bread at the table with them, and they heard him bless it as he'd done before. Their eyes were opened, and they recognized Jesus in that shared common meal.

In prison, Holy Communion may rarely be offered in the way it is in churches. But the Bible is full of stories of meals where the common becomes holy: There are miracles of manna in the wilderness, and feeding thousands with a few loaves and fishes. There are parables about banquets with poor folks and outcasts, and a parent hosting a feast for a wayward child. And there are moments of stunning awareness of Christ's presence, like that evening meal with travelers in Emmaus. In the same way—even most certainly in prison—whether at a service of Holy Communion or in sharing a common meal at chow, wherever two or three are gathered in Jesus' name, he is present.

A Quote to Ponder
I want the holiness of the Eucharist to spill out beyond the church walls, out of the hands of priests and into the regular streets and sidewalks, into the hands of regular, grubby people like you and me, onto our tables, in our kitchens and dining rooms and backyards. —Shauna Niequist[32]

A Question to Wonder About

Where have you seen Jesus breaking the bread, making the common holy, here in this place?

Prayer

Holy God, bring me to the table you have set for all of your creation. Bring me together with all your children of every race, nation, language, and identity to share the bread and wine that Jesus shared with his first disciples. Break open my heart in the breaking of the bread so that I might see through the false divisions created in this place and recognize your image in the faces of everyone. In Jesus' name I pray. Amen.

Song

Taste and See

> Taste and see, taste and see
> the goodness of the Lord.
> Oh, taste and see, taste and see
> the goodness of the Lord, of the Lord.
>
> I will bless the Lord at all times.
> Praise shall always be on my lips;
> my soul shall glory in the Lord;
> for God has been so good to me.[33]

—James E. Moore Jr., b. 1951, based on Ps. 34

BREAD FOR HUNGRY PEOPLE: PENTECOST

DAY OF PENTECOST: THE CHURCH'S FIRST SERMON

Mantra Prayer
Holy Fire has poured power upon us, and God is revealed in diversity. Come, Holy Spirit.

Scripture: Acts 2:1-6, 13, 14, 22b-24, 32-33, 36-39, 41
When the day of Pentecost had come, they were all together in one place. And suddenly from heaven there came a sound like the rush of a violent wind, and it filled the entire house where they were sitting. Divided tongues, as of fire, appeared among them, and a tongue rested on each of them. All of them were filled with the Holy Spirit and began to speak in other languages, as the Spirit gave them ability. Now there were devout Jews from every nation under heaven living in Jerusalem. And at this sound the crowd gathered and was bewildered, because each one heard them speaking in the native language of each. . . . All were amazed and perplexed, saying to one another, "What does this mean?" . . . But Peter, standing with the eleven, raised his voice and addressed them, "Men of Judea and all who live in Jerusalem, let this be known to you, and listen to what I say. . . . Jesus of Nazareth, a man attested to you by God with deeds of power, wonders, and signs that God did through him among you, as you yourselves know—this man, handed over to you according to the definite plan and foreknowledge of God, you crucified and killed by the hands of those outside the law. But God raised him up, having freed him from death, because it was impossible for him to be held in its power. . . . This Jesus God raised up, and of that all of us are witnesses. Being therefore exalted at the right hand of God, and having received from the Father the

Holy Spirit, Release Me with Your Fire

*You send forth your Spirit, and
they are created; and so you
renew the face of the earth.*

—*Psalm 104:30*

promise of the Holy Spirit, he has poured out this that you both see and hear.... Therefore let the entire house of Israel know with certainty that God has made him both Lord and Messiah, this Jesus whom you crucified." Now when they heard this, they were cut to the heart and said to Peter and to the other apostles, "Brothers, what should we do?" Peter said to them, "Repent, and be baptized every one of you in the name of Jesus Christ so that your sins may be forgiven; and you will receive the gift of the Holy Spirit. For the promise is for you, for your children, and for all who are far away, everyone whom the Lord our God calls to him."... So those who welcomed his message were baptized, and that day about three thousand persons were added.

Reflection

Pentecost is about the birth of the church, and the season that follows Pentecost Sunday is the longest in the church calendar. The Pentecost event in the scripture reading comes at a time when the disciples are confused, afraid, and leaderless. They recently watched Jesus be arrested by law enforcement and executed publicly. Though he came back to life, he left again, just a few weeks later. They aren't sure what fate awaits them if they continue to be his followers. Prison? Death? Or perhaps something completely amazing?

Prison is a place of forced diversity and integration, yet prison politics often segregate people into neat little groups that rarely interact on any real level. Being locked up also forces us to be around people from all over the cultural experience, perhaps for the first time in our lives. This can seem dangerous, but scripture paints a different picture. Maybe the diversity that seems so problematic while inside is actually part of God's plan for you and for the whole church.

In this reading from the book of Acts, as the disciples gather in community and try to lay low, the Holy Spirit is poured on them. Suddenly this group is the center of attention as they start declaring the word of God in all different languages. God intentionally chooses diversity of culture to start the first the church!

Suddenly empowered, Peter—who less than two months earlier had denied he was even a follower of Jesus—now stands and delivers the first public sermon in church history. Within this short sermon is almost the entire teaching of the Christian movement and message. Peter says, "This Jesus, whom you put to death—God raised him up! All of us are witnesses to that! And now he sits at the right hand of God, and he has poured out the Holy Spirit! That is what you are seeing and hearing!" Peter's words could have led to his imprisonment (and eventually, they do). But empowered by the Holy Spirit, Peter boldly declares the gospel message—that salvation has come, and you don't have to do anything to earn it. The entire deed has been done by Jesus of Nazareth.

A Quote to Ponder
Wherever the early Christians entered a town the power structure got disturbed and immediately sought to convict them for being "disturbers of the peace" and "outside agitators." But they went on with the conviction that they were "a colony of heaven" and had to obey God rather than man. They were small in number but big in commitment.
—The Rev. Dr. Martin Luther King Jr.[34]

A Question to Wonder About
What helps you recognize that the same power that gave birth to the church and launched the greatest social movements in human history is empowering you now?

Prayer

Holy Spirit, you flow through the lives of believers every day. You fill us with your fire, strengthen us during times of adversity, and gather us in community. For all this and more, I thank you. Holy Spirit, we are imperfect vessels in imperfect circumstances. Enter into our lives in this place. Empower me to carry the gospel message in my walk, my life, and my time in this place. In Jesus' name I pray. Amen.

Song

There Is a Balm in Gilead

> There is a balm in Gilead to make the wounded whole;
> there is a balm in Gilead to heal the sin-sick soul.
>
> Sometimes I feel discouraged and think my work's in vain,
> but then the Holy Spirit revives my soul again.
>
> African American spiritual

TIME AFTER PENTECOST 1: BURIED BROKENNESS

Mantra Prayer

I have been buried in my brokenness and raised in God's wholeness.
My brokenness is buried and my wholeness is holy.
My brokenness is buried and my wholeness has risen.

Scripture: Romans 6:1-11

What then are we to say? Should we continue in sin in order that grace may abound? By no means! How can we who died to sin go on living in it? Do you not know that all of us who have been baptized into Christ Jesus were baptized into his death?

Therefore we have been buried with him by baptism into death, so that, just as Christ was raised from the dead by the glory of the Father, so we too might walk in newness of life. For if we have been united with him in a death like his, we will certainly be united with him in a resurrection like his. We know that our old self was crucified with him so that the body of sin might be destroyed, and we might no longer be enslaved to sin. For whoever has died is freed from sin. But if we have died with Christ, we believe that we will also live with him. We know that Christ, being raised from the dead, will never die again; death no longer has dominion over him. The death he died, he died to sin, once for all; but the life he lives, he lives to God. So you also must consider yourselves dead to sin and alive to God in Christ Jesus.

Reflection

In this reading from Romans, we are confronted with what the power of grace really means. It means that Jesus went down to the very depths of death. But after his arrest by law enforcement and his execution by the state, he rose from the dead. His resurrection brings with it certain guarantees of new life that were given to you in baptism or are waiting for you at the baptismal font. No matter who you are, or what you have done or left undone, in baptism you get a gift from God. It is freely given and doesn't have to be earned.

What about the patterns of brokenness that we seem to live out in our lives? How are we to change the things that seem to rule over us and leave us no means of escape? In the scripture above, we get this incredible promise: "We know that our old self was crucified with [Jesus] so that the body of sin might be destroyed, and we might no longer be enslaved to sin."

The old self is gone, so why do we sometimes end up in jackpots still? The kingdom of God that Jesus initiated is at the same time here and not yet fully here. We exist in a world where we are sinner and saint at the exact same time. This explains why we are all capable of incredible acts of goodness as well as incredible acts of brokenness that cause pain for each other. But the promise of the cross and resurrection of Jesus is that we are no longer enslaved to sin. We are set free to love our neighbors and to invite Christ closer into our hearts, to help us break these cycles in our lives that aren't life-giving.

A Quote to Ponder

Imagine this tired old world when love is the way, unselfish, sacrificial, redemptive.

When love is the way, then no child will go to bed hungry in this world ever again.

When love is the way, we will let justice roll down like a mighty stream and righteousness like an ever-flowing brook.

When love is the way, poverty will become history.

When love is the way, the earth will be a sanctuary.

When love is the way, we will lay down our swords and shields, down by the riverside, to study war no more.

When love is the way, there's plenty good room, plenty good room, for all of God's children.

—Bishop Michael Curry[35]

A Question to Wonder About

How have you seen Jesus showing up to break your jackpots and lead you toward a better way of life?

Prayer

Jesus, you are the breaker of chains, and you are the one who has declared freedom to the prisoner. I ask that you help me recognize in what ways I am not serving you. Protect me in times of doubt. Show me how I can follow you more closely, so that I can live for the sake of the world. In Jesus' name I pray. Amen.

Song
We Shall Overcome

> We shall overcome, we shall overcome,
> we shall overcome someday.
> Oh, deep in our hearts we do believe
> we shall overcome someday.
>
> We'll walk hand in hand ...
> We shall all have peace ...
> We shall see the Lord ...
> We are not afraid ...
> God is on our side ...
> Traditional

TIME AFTER PENTECOST 2: RISKY TRUTH

Mantra prayer
I see God in the eyes of my neighbor when I get close enough to serve them.

Scripture: Mark 12:28-34
One of the scribes came near and heard them disputing with one another, and seeing that [Jesus] answered them well, he asked him, "Which commandment is the first of all?" Jesus

answered, "The first is, 'Hear, O Israel: the Lord our God, the Lord is one; you shall love the Lord your God with all your heart, and with all your soul, and with all your mind, and with all your strength.' The second is this, 'You shall love your neighbor as yourself.' There is no other commandment greater than these." Then the scribe said to him, "You are right, Teacher; you have truly said that 'he is one, and besides him there is no other'; and 'to love him with all the heart, and with all the understanding, and with all the strength,' and 'to love one's neighbor as oneself,'—this is much more important than all whole burnt offerings and sacrifices." When Jesus saw that he answered wisely, he said to him, "You are not far from the kingdom of God." After that no one dared to ask him any question.

Reflection

Rejoice! We have been set free! Even in circumstances where freedom seems to be a fleeting concept. Even in situations where just the word *freedom* seems to taunt us. But the truth is that we have been set free by the events at the cross. Through Jesus, we are given access to the incredible reality that every day, the kingdom of God is slipping into this world.

Freedom is risky inside just like it is outside.

When the scribe asked Jesus about the commandments, it was meant to be a trick. The scribe wanted to ensnare Jesus in an argument about the laws of Moses and to highlight the laws that the Pharisees were convinced Jesus wasn't following. (In Jesus' time, the Pharisees were a religious group who strictly observed the Law and Jewish ceremonies.) You see, the idea of loving neighbor, period, was a radical idea then, just like it is now.

Love is risky in a place where love is considered a weakness.

Think about it: If you started to build a community based on this principle of loving neighbor, could it stand up to the pressure of present circumstances? Is this a pie-in-the-sky idea, a nice target to aim for in life, but never really hit? Or is it a way of living that could radically change the atmosphere around us?

The truth is risky in a place where lies are the everyday currency.

The truth is that the love of God is only ever seen by the world around us in the way we love our neighbor. There is no exclusion clause to this, no certain kind of neighbor to love. God's love is spilled out on everyone regardless of their race, age, sexual identity, gender identity, or what they have done up until the moment you are reading this and even beyond. That's the amazing thing about the power of God's love: it is limitless. A passionate love affair with God is a passionate love affair with the vulnerable in your community.

A Quote to Ponder
To be a Christian means to forgive the inexcusable, because God has forgiven the inexcusable in you. —C. S. Lewis[36]

A Question to Wonder About
What's at risk if you try to love your neighbor here? What's at risk if you don't?

Prayer
God of love, reveal yourself in my community. No community is perfect, and not every neighbor is like me, but in that incredible exchange of your love and my service to others, through relationship building, I get to walk in your kingdom. In Jesus' name I pray. Amen.

Song
What a Fellowship, What a Joy Divine

> What a fellowship, what a joy divine,
> leaning on the everlasting arms;
> what a blessedness, what a peace is mine,
> leaning on the everlasting arms.
>
> Leaning, leaning,
> safe and secure from all alarms;
> leaning, leaning,
> leaning on the everlasting arms.
>
> Elisha F. Hoffman, 1839-1929

TIME AFTER PENTECOST 3: DAILY BREAD IS IMPORTANT TO THE HUNGRY

Mantra prayer
Life giver and creator, you are my breath and strength to go on.
Life-giving creator, you are God, and I can feel you when
    I breathe.

Scripture: Luke 11:1-4, 9-13
[Jesus] was praying in a certain place, and after he had
finished, one of his disciples said to him, "Lord, teach us to
pray, as John taught his disciples." He said to them, "When you
pray, say:
Father, hallowed be your name.
Your kingdom come.
Give us each day our daily bread.
And forgive us our sins,
for we ourselves forgive everyone indebted to us.
And do not bring us to the time of trial. . . .

"So I say to you, Ask, and it will be given you; search, and you will find; knock, and the door will be opened for you. For everyone who asks receives, and everyone who searches finds, and for everyone who knocks, the door will be opened. Is there anyone among you who, if your child asks for a fish, will give a snake instead of a fish? Or if the child asks for an egg, will give a scorpion? If you then, who are evil, know how to give good gifts to your children, how much more will the heavenly Father give the Holy Spirit to those who ask him!"

Reflection

How do we pray? What does it mean that Jesus uses this example that we call the "Lord's Prayer"? What is the power behind these words? Is it just these words, or is Jesus pointing to a greater truth? Maybe it's not just these words, but it's the form they take. Naming who God is: our Creator, in heaven, in glory, in power, in a realm well beyond what we can see, but a promised place for us all here and now, and in a future time. God's name is beyond all other names, and that name has given us this day, no matter where we are or what we have done.

We can't just pray our way out of difficulties. As you read this, you are probably thinking of all that lies ahead of you, the challenges that seem stacked against you to intentionally cause you to fail. But prayer empowers us to do the impossible. Once we receive that power, it's up to us to start walking down a road that is still difficult and at times narrow.

Today is our gift. This same God knows our struggles, so we ask for bread or whatever things we need, because this is a God who knows struggle and pain. This God who is Jesus knows hunger, sweat, betrayal, a mother's embrace, arrest, and trial. We ask for forgiveness, not because it's conditional, but because we are living out that grace and we are acknowledging what has already come to pass. Though times of trial come and go, this same Jesus is forever. Prayer and petitions are like rubbing God's ears with God's promises, holding God to account for God's promises to us. To remind God of the promises God makes to us in baptism and in the gospel. That is what prayer is like.

A Quote to Ponder

With all other blessings sought at the mercy seat, I always prayed that God would, of [God's] great mercy, and in [God's] own good time, deliver me from my bondage. —Frederick Douglass[37]

A Question to Wonder About

Have you ever asked Jesus how he would like you to pray?

Prayer: The Lord's Prayer

Our Father in heaven, hallowed be your name, your kingdom come, your will be done, on earth as in heaven. Give us today our daily bread. Forgive us our sins as we forgive those who sin against us. Save us from the time of trial and deliver us from evil. For the kingdom, the power, and the glory are yours, now and forever. Amen.

Song

It's Me, O Lord

> It's me, it's me, O Lord, standin' in the need of prayer;
> it's me, it's me, O Lord, standin' in the need of prayer.
>
> Not the stranger, not my neighbor, but it's me, O Lord, standin' in the need of prayer;
> not the stranger, not my neighbor, but it's me, O Lord, standin' in the need of prayer.
>
> African American spiritual

TIME AFTER PENTECOST 4: FINDING PEACE IN A TROUBLED WORLD

Mantra Prayer
Empires rise and empires fall, but Jesus stands always in the midst. I am welcome.

Scripture: Luke 21:10-19
Then [Jesus] said to them, "Nation will rise against nation, and kingdom against kingdom; there will be great earthquakes, and in various places famines and plagues; and there will be dreadful portents and great signs from heaven. But before all this occurs, they will arrest you and persecute you; they will hand you over to synagogues and prisons, and you will be brought before kings and governors because of my name. This will give you an opportunity to testify. So make up your minds not to prepare your defense in advance; for I will give you words and a wisdom that none of your opponents will be able to withstand or contradict. You will be betrayed even by parents and brothers, by relatives and friends; and they will put some of you to death. You will be hated by all because of my name. But not a hair of your head will perish. By your endurance you will gain your souls."

Reflection
What does it mean that we experience times of trial? In the Lord's Prayer we ask God to "save us from the time of trial." Does that mean we won't ever experience hard times? Well, our experience in this world shouts, "No, that's not true at all!" In fact, as we journey through life, it's easy to listen to all the noise and to believe that this world is nothing but hard times, broken promises, and justice long delayed, if not denied. Jesus Christ warns of days when it will feel like the entire world is rising up to destroy itself, and he gives a bold promise: "But not

a hair of your head will perish. By your endurance you will gain your souls."

The cost of salvation has been paid, so it's important to note that that isn't what Jesus is talking about. Instead, it's the way we turn to Jesus and throw ourselves on his mercy and care in times of great trial—that's how we gain our souls. Our souls are woven into a bigger tapestry that stretches well beyond the walls we sit within. We are knitted together with millions of other believers across the world. We are all connected to this power called Jesus. You are connected to this power called Jesus, and through him, you are able to endure any trial. Even if nation should rise against nation, and false prophets rise selling hate as if it were love, even so, we will all endure and overcome, through God's grace.

A Quote to Ponder
I am fundamentally an optimist. Whether that comes from nature or nurture, I cannot say. Part of being optimistic is keeping one's head pointed toward the sun, one's feet moving forward. There were many dark moments when my faith in humanity was sorely tested, but I would not and could not give myself up to despair. That way lay defeat and death.
—Nelson Mandela[38]

A Question to Wonder About
Do you really trust that Jesus can protect you, no matter the state of your personal world or the wider one?

Prayer
Liberating One, remind me that I can endure—no matter the trial, the weight of my plight, or the rulers of this world; no matter if every official stands in my way. I am assured of liberation because I follow you, and you have declared my

freedom. In the name of the one who endured to the end and set me free, Jesus Christ of Nazareth. Amen.

Song
I'm So Glad Jesus Lifted Me

> I'm so glad Jesus lifted me.
> I'm so glad Jesus lifted me.
> I'm so glad Jesus lifted me,
> singing glory, hallelujah! Jesus lifted me.
>
> When I was in trouble, Jesus lifted me ...
> African American spiritual

Come, Loving/Liberating God

Likewise the Spirit helps us in our weakness; for we do not know how to pray as we ought, but that very Spirit intercedes with sighs too deep for words.

—*Romans 8:26*

PRAYING THROUGH ORDINARY DAYS

PRAYERS FOR SPECIFIC SITUATIONS: SEEKING GOD IN ALL THINGS

Before sentencing

Redeeming God, I do not know what lies ahead. I ask that all who will be hearing my case and deciding my fate consider all of the evidence and weigh it fairly. I ask that they have open minds and understand that I am so much more than a list of charges. I ask for strength and patience for myself, my family, and all who love and support me as we figure out what the future looks like. Gracious God, I know that you are always with me. Help me to feel your presence, especially at this time. I ask this in the name of Jesus. Amen.

Before court

God of justice, once again I must stand before an imperfect court and a human judge. I cannot put my hope in them, but I embrace the promise that your justice and your mercy will prevail. Let righteousness and peace embrace this day, and bring justice to my cause. In Jesus' name I pray. Amen.

Public humiliation

God of the humiliated and downtrodden, you were a prisoner, bound and paraded in front of others. Do you know how it is for me? Not the chain belting my waist, the shackles binding my ankles, or the cuffs tight on my wrists: these are not the worst. It is the humiliation I feel when eyes stare at me and then quickly look away in avoidance. I dread my trips outside the shield of prison, where I become a curiosity and target for ridicule. See me through these times. Help me trust your love for me and believe in my own worth and dignity. I ask this in the name of Jesus. Amen.

Humiliating rules

God of order, Jesus saw a paralyzed man, forgave his sins, and then told him to stand up and walk. The authorities who watched didn't understand and objected to his mercy. Here in prison, it feels like we are paralyzed too. So many rules just keep us down: they're always changing with no notice. We can't know what to expect. We don't know when we will be punished or belittled for reasons we don't understand. Give me the hope and strength I need to endure humiliation, and help me to stand and walk. I ask this in the name of Jesus. Amen.

Lockdown

Jesus of freedom, some of your own disciples, like Peter and John and Paul and many other followers since then—and even you—have been held in prison and not known what was happening outside, how long the doors would be locked, or if they would ever be opened. But even trapped in prison, those who trusted you found a way to live with hope and freedom. Help me to have that same freedom that you give and that they knew. Grant me the spirit I need to find joy while inside these fences and walls. I ask this in your holy name. Amen.

Solitary confinement

O God, you promised that you are with us wherever we go and that there is no place where we can flee from your presence. I claim that promise right here and now. Help me to feel you with me here in solitary. Help me to know that as long as I am yours, there is no place where I am beyond your reach. Remind me that you will never leave me or forsake me. Give me the strength and courage to face this time and to use the quiet to calm my spirit and focus my attention on your grace and care. I pray in the name of your Son, Jesus Christ. Amen.

So much noise

God of the still, small voice: I am exhausted beyond control by all the noise. Dominoes hammer on tables outside my cell door. Flat palms slap poker cards with tornado force. Televisions stutter full-volume echoes against concrete walls. Metal doors slam from morning's first count until the last one at night. Static vibrates from radios. Shouting spills out of showers. Announcements boom over voice-distorting speakers. Chairs make crash-landing collisions. Alarms screech. . . . The relentless noise punishes me until I want to scream a demand for silence that never comes. Dear God, in all this endless noise, grant me quiet rest. I ask this in the name of Jesus. Amen.

Transfer to another facility

God in all places, I may be transferred to another prison. I've figured out how to get along where I am. I know what to count on here, who the guards are, what I can and cannot do, who to trust and who not to trust. I'm sad to say goodbye to friends who have been part of my life here. Moving may be good, but it makes me nervous. Who will be in the cell with me? Will I have a job? Can I have visits? Will I be able to bring my things with me? I've done this before; help me do it again. I ask this in the name of Jesus. Amen.

My recent return to incarceration
Forgiving and liberating God, I have made poor choices. The world beyond these walls overwhelmed me at times. I didn't fully understand the rules I needed to follow while on parole. I admit that I was not prepared for the challenges and barriers I encountered, and now I find myself back in prison. God, my refuge and strength, I pray for a calm spirit. I pray for the desire and commitment to prepare for life outside these walls and to encourage others here with me. I pray that I will truly know that this loss of liberty does not mean loss of freedom because in you, Living God, I have freedom that no one can take away from me. I know that by your healing grace and mercy, I will make it through with the help of Jesus. Amen.

For my family as I return to incarceration
God our strength, now that I'm back in prison, I worry for my family. I regret that I have disappointed them and that I am not there for them. Meet their needs and give them comfort and protection. Assure them of the healing and wholeness you give to make it through each and every day. In Jesus' name I pray. Amen.

Parenting from prison
Nurturing God, I feel so helpless and like a failure, being a parent in prison. What can I do for my [children/daughter/son] from here? So much time together is gone. We are too much like strangers, not knowing each other, or sharing life, or showing love. Special days are missed. I feel the anger because I'm not there, and I wonder who is. Will I have the chance to make it up or be forgiven? I'm praying for that chance. I ask this in the name of Jesus. Amen.

Preparing for a family visit

God of love and hope, as I prepare for my visit today, I am grateful. This environment is not easy to take, even on the best day, so visits are important and greatly appreciated. Thank you, God, for family and friends who graciously spend their time and money to visit me. Their support and love give me the determination and strength to continue moving forward. I ask that they will be safe while traveling and that our visit will be filled with joy and love. In Jesus' name I pray. Amen.

Loneliness

O God, somewhere: It is so lonely here—this is the worst of it for me. I am so lonely, cut off, far away. My companion is loneliness every day and night. I wait for mail, I linger at the phone, I dream of a visit, I miss being touched. There is so much noise, so many people all around, but I am all alone. Wherever you are, help me believe that you hear me and that I am not forgotten. Be with me, God. I ask this in the name of Jesus. Amen.

All alone

Jesus, who prepares a home: You said that foxes have holes and birds have nests but that you had nowhere, so I think you know how it is for me. I get no visits and no letters. I have no one to call and no place to go when I leave prison. Mostly, I feel empty and unwanted. I know I made mistakes and caused people to turn away from me. But, please, don't you desert me. Help me find my place, and show me where I belong. I ask this in your holy name. Amen.

Missing nature

God of creation, the beauty of your world seems so far from here. There is so little of the natural world in prison. Seasons don't much entertain us. Lilacs flower in spring and maples

drop leaves in autumn, but we don't smell their fragrance
or see their color. The sun rises and sets over days lived
under horizons of guard towers and walls. I imagine borders
of evergreen and see hedges of razor wire. Help me to be
thankful for all the beauty of nature always: here where it is
so sparse, and also in future days when I am free and it will be
so obviously abundant. I ask this in the name of Jesus. Amen.

Disappointment

Jesus, I dared to think of a better future, only to be denied. I
raised my hopes, only to have them thrown down. When will
your saving help come to me? When will your justice prevail?
Suffering Jesus, you also have been denied. You have been
thrown down. You have known injustice. Come to me now and
walk with me through this dark valley. Comfort me in my
disappointment, and raise up in me a hope that will not be
shaken. I ask this in your holy name. Amen.

Anger

God of storm and calm, you reveal your own anger at injustice
and all that brings harm, and where there is fury and offense,
you show the way to peace. There is so much anger within
and all around me. Help me to know and find the right use of
anger, and free me from its power to enslave or misguide me,
so that I may follow your way of justice and mercy. I ask this in
the name of Jesus. Amen.

Depression

Lord of hope, I am so depressed, sinking where even my own
shadow won't stay by me. I don't know where to go, how to get
help, or what to do. There is no one here that I trust. I'm afraid.
I'm so tired of all this. I'm ready to give up. Is there help for
me? Send me help. Lift me out of this heavy fog. Is there any

hope? Show me a reason to hope. Don't give up on me. I ask this in the name of Jesus. Amen.

Fear

Almighty and powerful God, today I am afraid. I just feel scared. Sometimes I'm not even sure why. There are lots of reasons: Fights and ridicule. Cell searches, tickets, predators, thieves and snitches and cons. Guards that don't like me, bad news in the mail, nowhere for me to go when I get out. I don't know why—today I'm just scared. Make me strong enough and give me the courage to get through this. Help me. I ask this in the name of Jesus. Amen.

Assaulted in prison

God, my refuge and my protector: You know what is happening to me here—the attacks. I feel weak and ashamed. I'm angry and sad and so afraid. This is a brutal place. I can't get away from the threats, the looks, and the bullying. I'm a target who can't breathe. I have no safe hiding place. Give me courage to get through this. Protect me, save me from this hell. I ask this in the name of Jesus. Amen.

Mental health

God of heart, mind, and soul: It's hard for me to think clearly. I worry, I'm afraid, and I'm angry. Sleeping is a problem. The medicines they give me make me feel awful. I know something is wrong with me. I need help, but I fear that if I tell anyone, they won't care or they might use it against me. Help me know what to do. Calm me down, untangle this confusion, drive out my dark thoughts like you chased away bad spirits. I ask this in the name of Jesus. Amen.

Thoughts of suicide

God, who gave me life: Didn't Judas kill himself when he thought his life wasn't worth living? I know how that is. A lot of the time I feel like I've had too much and can take no more. I feel like I don't matter to anyone and have no future. What's the use of living like this? I don't want to live, and I don't want to die. Please take these thoughts away. Keep me safe. Show me a way to find something worth holding on to. I ask this in the name of Jesus. Amen.

Health issues

God who heals, you cured many people with all kinds of diseases—I don't know, maybe you still do. I need help. I am sick, I'm in pain, and I'm scared. It's miserable not to feel well in prison. Medical help is hard to get, and it's not very good. Help me stay strong, relieve my pain, send the care I need, and help me to be healthy. I ask this in the name of Jesus. Amen.

Birthday in prison

God of passing years, Psalm 90 says, "Teach us to count our days that we may gain a wise heart." Birthdays in prison are hard. The days and years of my life are passing by, and I am stuck. Time is wasted. Each birthday is a reminder of how much I've thrown away. Help me to value every day of my life, to use this time and all that is ahead of me well. Guide me past the regrets over time gone, and help me find meaning and happiness in each new day of grace. I ask this in the name of Jesus. Amen.

Growing old in prison

God of the ages, the prospect of growing old and of my life maybe even ending in prison is not easy for me to accept. I grieve over all that could have been, over what I wish my life could be like now. I worry about poor health, how my body will weaken, and the discomforts of prison becoming even more difficult. I mourn the vanishing hopes for another chapter of life beyond prison. Help me to seek and make peace, to find contentment, and to receive your grace for this time in my life. I ask this in the name of Jesus. Amen.

Dying in prison
God of beginnings and endings, I am dying. I will not live to leave prison. I am far beyond any of the places of sadness I've ever known. I am afraid and very alone. All I can hope for is enough strength to face what is ahead, for relief from pain, for kindness near me while I die, and for forgiveness for my sins. Have mercy on me as Jesus had mercy for the dying thief on the cross beside him when he promised, "Today you will be with me in Paradise." This I ask in the name of Jesus. Amen.

Death row
Lord Jesus Christ, you know from your own life what it's like to be arrested, tried, and sentenced to death. Thank you for the example of courage that you give. Be powerfully present with me on death row. Calm my fears and still my dread. Be my friend and companion as I wait and watch and worry. As you opened the door to paradise for the thief on the cross next to you, please open the gateway to resurrection and life in you when my day of death comes. Hear my cry, O Lord, and listen to my plea. I ask this in your holy name. Amen.

Guilt
God of justice, you know the guilt that I carry. You know the hurt I have caused. You know the harm I have done. You know the heaviness I hold. And I know, too, what has brought judgment upon me. I confess my sin, and I ask you to guide my life in the direction Jesus leads me. I ask this in the name of Jesus. Amen.

For forgiveness

Merciful God, I have sinned in ways that I know and do not know. I have offended and harmed others, and I have brought trouble upon myself. I am sorry for what I have done that is wrong and for not doing what is right. I ask for this: that you forgive my sins, that I find forgiveness from those against whom I have sinned, that you help me forgive others, and that you help me forgive myself. I ask this in the name of Jesus. Amen.

Show me the way

Ever-knowing God, from your wisdom and out of your compassion, show me a right and holy way to live. Teach me to be patient and kind, forgiving and generous, thankful and truthful. Give me the will, the wisdom, the courage, and the faith to trust and follow you. I ask this in the name of Jesus. Amen.

Joy

God of life, this is a good day. My heart is light, and I am holding on to hope and good news. I'm blessed in ways I did not expect, and there is joy in my life, even here. Is this a miracle? It feels like it is. I pray that this joy will not be mine alone. Whatever is ahead, give me joy in your goodness and mercy. I ask this in the name of Jesus. Amen.

Hard to feel thankful

Generous God, it can be hard in here to be thankful or to feel grateful. It's so easy to hang low, all sorry for myself, feeling cheated in life, bitter about being locked up. So, when I'm feeling this way and can't see the good, when I don't notice your blessings, forgive me. Open my eyes, unblock my ears, and guide my attention so that I may not miss the greatness

of your love and fail to give thanks. I ask this in the name of
Jesus. Amen.

Thanksgiving
God of creation, thank you for all the gifts of creation and
for the blessings of life through day and night. Thank you for
the good that has been, the mercies you are showing me now,
and the hope for tomorrow. As you bless my life, may I reflect
your grace and be a blessing to others. I ask this in the name of
Jesus. Amen.

Prayers for meals
Come, Lord Jesus, be our guest, and let *thy/your/these* gifts
to us be blessed. Blessed be God, who is our bread; may all the
world be clothed and fed. Amen.[39]

Bless, O Lord, your gifts to our use and us to your service; for
Christ's sake. Amen.[40]

God of creation, it can be hard to be grateful for meals in
prison. I miss foods from my family, foods that remind me of
good times, foods that delight me. Even in this place, make me
mindful of those whose tables are empty, of those who grow
our food, and of the ways we depend upon the resources of the
land. Amen.

A cry
A voice says, "Cry out!" And I said, "What shall I cry?"
Crying for children who grow up without parents.
Crying for past wrongs and unjust treatments.
Crying for a sense of belonging and being loved.
Crying for forgiveness and reconciliation.
Crying for community, when feeling all alone.

And amidst our cries, God gathers us, names us, and loves us as God's very own, without ever growing weary. God will renew our strength and help us meet another day. Amen.

Times of financial stress

God of abundance, I am stressed about money. I want to call family and friends, and that takes money. I need toiletries and personal items, but that takes money. Gracious God, the list could go on and on. It is difficult to stay connected to the world outside and to the people who are my support system when I lack money. I ask for guidance and a positive attitude so that I do not worry about money or become resentful when it does not arrive when I want it to. I ask for a mind-set that will help me appreciate those who make sacrifices to provide for me financially. Please help me be ever mindful of those in circumstances much worse than my own and who must go without the basic necessities for living. In Jesus' name I pray. Amen.

For recovery from addiction

God, give us grace to accept with serenity the things that cannot be changed, courage to change the things that should be changed, and the wisdom to distinguish the one from the other: living one day at a time, enjoying one moment at a time, accepting hardship as a pathway to peace; taking, as Jesus did, this sinful world as it is, not as we would have it; trusting that you will make all things right, if we surrender to your will; so that we may be reasonably happy in this life, and supremely happy with you forever in the next. Amen.[41]

Preparation for leaving prison

Creator of the universe, I am thankful for this part of my journey, and I know that you have been with me every step of the way. I am anxious about what is to come as I begin the next chapter. I am sad to leave behind many people and things that mean so much to me. I know that there will be challenges ahead and many new things to learn. I ask that you give me an open mind and a gentle spirit so that I may see your Spirit at work in me as I learn to walk in the new life that awaits me on the other side of these walls. In Jesus' name I pray. Amen.

No work skills

God of purpose, the Bible says it is good to eat and drink and find enjoyment in the work we do for our lives. When I leave prison, it will be hard to get a job. I'm a felon with hardly any training, no experience, and not much education. Who will hire me? How will I make a living? I want to build a new life and stay away from crime, but I don't know where to begin. I pray for someone to give me a chance. I pray to learn a skill, to just get a start. Help me find work that I can do and a future to enjoy. I ask this in the name of Jesus. Amen.

Homeless upon release from prison

God of our future, I am leaving prison and I have no place to go, nowhere to live. I will be homeless. There is no one waiting for me. I am scared of being on the streets and anxious about being all alone. I am afraid of what will happen to me. You say not to worry about tomorrow, about life, about what to eat or drink or wear. You say to trust that you will provide for daily needs. That's hard for me. Please watch over me. Help me to stay out of trouble and not to come back to prison. Help me to thrive and make a new life for myself. I ask it in the name of Jesus. Amen.

When leaving prison

O God, you have called me to ventures of which I cannot see the ending, by paths as yet untrodden, through perils unknown. Give me faith to go out with good courage, not knowing where

I go, but only that your hand is leading me and your love supporting me; through Jesus Christ our Lord. Amen.[42]

A prayer of Patrick (c. 389–461)
Christ be with me, Christ before me, Christ behind me,
Christ within me, Christ beneath me, Christ above me,
Christ on my right, Christ on my left,
Christ where I lie, Christ where I sit, Christ where I arise,
Christ in the heart of everyone who thinks of me,
Christ in the mouth of everyone who speaks of me,
Christ in every eye that sees me,
Christ in every ear that hears me;
for salvation is of Christ the Lord.
Let your salvation, O Lord, be ever with us. Amen.[43]

A prayer of Augustine of Hippo (354–430)
O loving God, to turn away from you is to fall, to turn toward you is to rise, and to stand before you is to abide forever. Grant us, dear God, in all our duties your help; in all our uncertainties your guidance; in all our dangers your protection, and in all our sorrows your peace; through Jesus Christ our Lord. Amen.[44]

A prayer attributed to Francis of Assisi (1182–1286)
Lord, make us instruments of your peace. Where there is hatred, let us sow love; where there is injury, pardon; where there is discord, union; where there is doubt, faith; where there is despair, hope; where there is darkness, light; where there is sadness, joy. Grant that we may not so much seek to be consoled as to console; to be understood as to understand; to be loved as to love. For it is in giving that we receive; it is in pardoning that we are pardoned; and it is in dying that we are born to eternal life. Amen.[45]

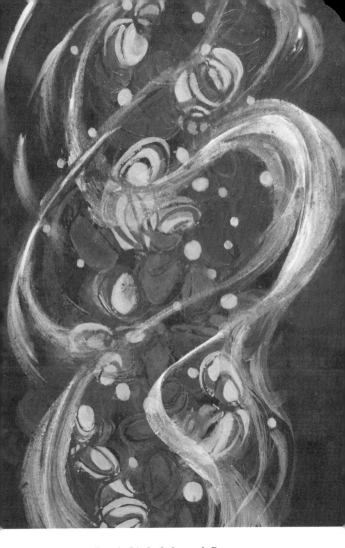

People Linked through Prayer

Beloved, let us love one another,
because love is from God.

—1 John 4:7

PRAYERS FOR OTHERS: SEEING GOD IN ONE ANOTHER

For my cellmate

Gracious God, in these cells we live inches from one another hour by hour, month by month. Inspire me to see my cellmate, _name_, as a child of God created in your image and loved by you just as I am loved. When we need it, give us patience. When we lack it, provide understanding. When there is fault, teach us to be forgiving. In discord, grant fair resolution; in shortage, generosity; in worry, encouragement; and in need, support. I ask this in the name of Jesus. Amen.

For enemies

God of reconciliation, Jesus teaches us to love our enemies, to pray for them, and to do good even to those who hurt us. This is a hard teaching here, where we think of many as enemies. Show me, and all of us in prison, the power of your transforming love. Prevent acts of retribution, drive out destructive anger, and hinder the spirit of revenge. Give us the courage to follow where you lead. I ask this in the name of Jesus. Amen.

For friends

God among us, thank you for the gift of friends, those who have forgiven and loved me when I have not made it easy for them. Thank you for friends who stand by me and sacrifice for me, who show me support and give me encouragement. Help me in the same way to be a trustworthy friend to others, caring for their welfare and being worthy of their trust. Keep me from exploiting my friends. Keep me from failing to show gratitude for them. I ask this in the name of Jesus. Amen.

For gangs

God of community, show the way for us to live together as you desire—in harmony. Help us to find our support and acceptance and to make our allegiance in relationships that create goodwill and care for the welfare of others. Defeat the allure of gangs, where violence masquerades as security. Frustrate their muscling demands and discourage their efforts at coercive recruitment. Raise up and encourage honorable companions, and strengthen the bonds of kindliness among us all in this place. I ask this in the name of Jesus. Amen.

For other Christians

God of hope, I give you thanks for the whole communion of saints, my Christian siblings whose witness to your love reveals Jesus' way of mercy. I thank you for all those who bring me hope through discouraging times, who teach the word of God, and who strengthen my desire to live a life of peace and justice. Set free the saving message of the gospel's good news within these prison walls, and give heart and energy for the work of Christian compassion among us. I ask this in the name of Jesus. Amen.

For victims

God of healing, give recovery to those whom I have harmed and offended, to their families and friends, and to the communities and relationships where lives have been torn by my actions. Restore them to peace where it has crumbled, grant them safekeeping through the night and day, and provide relief from the injury I have caused. Console us all with your grace as you renew your whole creation. I ask this in the name of Jesus. Amen.

For chaplains and volunteers

God of grace, bless the chaplains and all the volunteers who teach and visit, counsel and console, that they receive joy and meaning in their ministry. Inspire each of them to be an example of your love, the voice of grace, the presence of wisdom, and an instrument of renewal. Keep them faithful to the gospel and make them bold in its proclamation. Assure them of the good fruits of their labor, and grant them fulfillment in their work. I ask this in the name of Jesus. Amen.

For corrections officers and prison staff

God of us all, I pray for those who work as officers and guards and for those who administer and staff the prison through day and night. Give them good judgment and healthy patience, and keep them worthy of respect. Keep them watchful and safe; sustain them in times of weariness and stress. Advance mutual consideration between those imprisoned and corrections officers to foster dignity and nurture human worth. When all we can see is the uniform, help us to see the individual who wears it. When they seem arbitrary or unfair, help us to be tolerant. When they are cruel, shield us. When they show commitment to our care and safety, help us to recognize it and be thankful. I ask this in the name of Jesus. Amen.

For law enforcement

God of promise, instill in me a right mind and a fair heart toward the police and those who work in law enforcement. Guard them in their labor and keep them secure from danger. Guide them in their duty, that they may safely protect the community while behaving rightly and with honor. Drive away all prejudice from their hearts, support them in all that is just, and impede what is not just. Help them to treat each

person they encounter with fairness, respect, and due process.
I ask this in the name of Jesus. Amen.

For lawyers and judges
God of justice, give guidance in our courts to those who define
and administer justice, that they may be worthy of the trust
given to them. Grant to lawyers and judges a full measure
of wisdom, care in deliberation, a right desire for truth, and
diligence in serving the common good. Cause them to make
their judgments with equity and impartiality toward each
person who comes before them. Do not let expedience displace
integrity. Do not let the powerful disadvantage the weak. And
in all matters, for those who accuse and those who defend,
those who judge and those who are judged, inspire humility
toward the truth and respect for the dignity of all. I ask this in
the name of Jesus. Amen.

For the diversity of people
O God of all, with wonderful diversity of languages and
cultures you created all people in your image. Free us from
prejudice and fear, that we may see your face in the faces of
people around the world; through Jesus Christ, our Savior and
Lord. Amen.[46]

For transformation of racism
Loving and liberating God, your Son, Jesus Christ, was taken
by law enforcement in the night when he was betrayed, was
railroaded in court, and was killed in a state-sanctioned
murder by execution. We know that there is still injustice in
this world and that something in direct opposition to your
kingdom is at the very heart of the present prison-industrial
complex. Help us confront it, name it, and cast it out of our
society. We name systemic racism as a sin that is abhorrent to
you. We name that the prison system and the legal system are

often tools of this same systemic racism. Remind us that just because something is legal, that does not mean it is of you. We call on you and your power to transform hearts and dismantle all systems of oppression, inequity, injustice, and racism in our penal system. In the name of Jesus we pray. Amen.

A prayer from Ravensbrück Concentration Camp—
written by an unknown prisoner and left by the body of a dead child.
Lord, remember not only the men and women of good will, but also those of ill will. But do not remember all the suffering they have inflicted upon us; remember the fruits we have brought, thanks to this suffering—our comradeship, our loyalty, our humility, our courage, our generosity, the greatness of heart which has grown out of all this, and when they come to judgment let all the fruits we have borne be their forgiveness.[47]

For prisons and correctional institutions
God of justice, for our sake your Son was condemned as a criminal. Visit our jails and prisons with your judgment and mercy. Remember all prisoners; bring the guilty to repentance and amendment of life according to your will; and give hope for the future. When any are held unjustly, raise up for them advocates to bring them release, and give us the wisdom to improve our system of justice. Watch over those who work in these institutions; give them strength and compassion and keep them from becoming brutal or callous. Lead us to do for those in prison what we would do for Christ, in whose name we pray. Amen.[48]

PRAYING INSIDE WITH THOSE OUTSIDE

Human beings are made for relationship. Yet, when daily interaction is cut off by incarceration, even our deepest relationships can suffer. A powerful way to combat the isolation is by mutual, shared prayer. Mutual, shared prayers are ones that both we and our family members or friends pray at the same time, even when we are apart.

Consider the prayer for the beginning of the day. How meaningful it would be to bless the ones we love with a prayer in the morning! And how comforting it would be to know they are blessing us with the same prayer at the very same time! Praying inside with those praying outside brings us closer to one another in spirit and keeps us in deep relationship.

We recommend that you arrange with your loved ones to pray one or more of these prayers for each other every day. The prayers at the beginning and end of the day might be the easiest to start with. As soon as you wake up, say the prayer. When you go to bed, say the prayer. They are intentionally brief so they can eventually be memorized. From there, other situations will call forth mutual prayer. Over time, this practice will remind you, through good times and bad, that neither you nor your loved ones are ever separated from God's love. It will also help you sense more strongly how God's love connects you with one another, even when you are apart. May God bless you and the ones you love through mutual, shared prayer.

Prayer at the beginning of the day
O Morning Star, again this day _name/s_ *are* waking up far away from me. Surround *them* with your love and remind *them*

of my love, too. Kiss *their* foreheads, guard *their* hearts, and strengthen *their* shoulders for the work of the day. Amen.

For parents and children
Dear God, I miss my *child/children/mother/father/spouse*, and it hurts that I can't hold *them* and embrace *them*. Sometimes it hurts so much that I have to push *them* out of my mind. But you, O God, are always mindful of *them*. Give *them* everything *they* need this day: health and joy and food for the day. May those who *watch over/work with/share the day with them* have kind and generous hearts, and may we all, at last, be gathered together into your loving embrace. Amen.

For missing milestones
O God, our times are in your hand. Look with favor on my *daughter/son/friend*, _name_, on this occasion of *their birth/ first step/birthday/graduation/other milestone*. My heart is grieved to be absent, and I pray that *they* may always know my love and my desire to be a part of *their* life; through Jesus Christ, our Savior and Lord. Amen.

At the loss of a loved one
Lord Jesus, you wept upon hearing the news of Lazarus's death, so I know you understand the grief I feel being absent at the death of my *friend/family member*. There are so many things I wish I could have said. I now lay those words before you, trusting that you hold *them* in the palm of your hand forevermore. Comfort me with the knowledge that you gather all the faithful into your presence. Amen.

For family/friends
Holy God, watch over and strengthen my *friend/parent/ spouse* today, who works so hard to hold everything together while I am away. *They* are a treasured blessing, and I give

you thanks for bringing *them* into my life. I entrust *them* into your unfailing care and look forward to the day we are reunited; through Jesus Christ our Lord. Amen.

Before a family visit
O God of peace, you know my desire to make up in one visit for all the time _name/s_ and I have been apart. You know my fear that we will fail. Give each of us peace, and keep me from pressing for more than the short time allows. Let us be fully present to you and to each other. Bless us with all that we need in our time together. Amen.

On special family occasions
O Holy Comforter, on this day of joy and celebration, feelings of disappointment and grief also arise because _name/s_ and I are apart. I thank you for this occasion, and I ask you to bless us, comfort us, and unite us in spirit until the day when we can celebrate together. Amen.

In time of family resentment
O God, we are filled with resentment and quick to blame those close to us for our current problems. Speak to our souls in this time of distress. Give us the courage to suffer what is ours to suffer and not put it on others. Bring us back to gracious love for one another. Amen.

In times of financial stress
O God of mercy, you know our family's hopes and desires. You know our poverty and our fear. Do not turn away from us, and do not let our hopes fail. Listen to our cries and give us relief in this time of need. Amen.

At the end of the day

O God, again tonight, *name/s are* going to bed far away from me. Bless *them* at the end of the day and give *them* rest. Kiss *their* foreheads, guard *their* hearts, and take from *their* shoulders the burdens of the day. Amen.

At all times

To be repeated silently throughout the day:
Lord, Jesus Christ, Son of God, have mercy on your *servant/s.*

At the loss of loved ones

God of the living and the dead,

I come to you at this time to grieve the loss of *name and/or relationship* and to offer my goodbye to *name/s*.

During this time, I give thanks for *their* life and what *their* presence in my life has meant to me.

Silence for reflection.

Being isolated from family and friends at this time is very difficult—I acknowledge that. Yet I know that you are with me, Loving God, and I trust that by the comfort of the Holy Spirit, I will be able to journey through this time of transition.

Silence for reflection.

Forgiving God, I have many regrets about the circumstances that have separated me from *name/s*. I am truly sorry for any hurt that I caused *them*. Today, I am grateful for your forgiveness. Please help me to lay aside my regrets.

There are things I need to say to _name/s_—things that I may never have said before. I will speak them aloud or in my heart and then I will let these things go, trusting that my intent is now known.

Speak whatever you need to speak to your loved one/s while you hold a picture of them (an actual picture or a mental one).

The loss of _name/relationship_ leaves an empty place in my heart and life. O God, I ask you to fill that place with all that I shared with *them* during life.

O God who eases pain, it is difficult to cry here. Tears are seen as weakness here, but I have tears I need to shed. Help me, God.

Silence for reflection.

Loving God, I thank you for the life of _name and/or relationship_ and for all the love _name_ gave to me.

Ever-present God, your Word tells me that there is a season for everything. Life and death are part of the unending circle of creation. The life of _name_ has come to an end. I will always hold *them* in my heart, and I entrust *them* to your eternal care.

I say goodbye and amen.

Pray without Ceasing

*The LORD grants lovingkindness
in the daytime; in the night
season the LORD's song is with me,
a prayer to the God of my life.*

—Psalm 42:8

PRAYING ALL DAY LONG

How to Use This Section

Morning Prayer, Evening Prayer, and Night Prayer are three ways to frame your day in prayer. This pattern is sometimes called "praying the hours." It has been done for centuries by Christians in groups or alone. Praying at various times of day is a practice shared by Christians, Jews, and Muslims.

Evening Prayer and Morning Prayer remind us of Christ's passage through death to resurrection. As evening comes, we look to the light of Christ that scatters all darkness. With the rising sun, we praise God for the resurrection of Jesus, and we ask the Holy Spirit to help us follow Jesus into another day. Night Prayer offers a time to acknowledge both the gifts and the failings of the day, and we place ourselves and the whole world into God's hands as we go to sleep.

Even if you are alone in a prison cell, you are joining in these prayers with other Christians around the world, across time zones and miles. You are also praying with Jesus' followers through the ages. Now they live and worship in the light of God's presence, but during their life on earth, many of them prayed these very prayers in their own language. How meaningful to pray in this way that connects us with so many other believers!

MORNING PRAYER

Opening

> This is the day that the Lord has made;
> I will rejoice and be glad in it.
>
> **OR**
>
> We rise and begin a new day, knowing that you, O God,
> are always with us. Open our eyes to your presence.

Psalmody

*You may read Psalm 63:1-8 (below) or one of your choosing
found in the "Selected Psalms" section (page 191).*

¹O God, you are my God; eagerly I seek you;
> my soul thirsts for you, my flesh faints for you,
> > as in a dry and weary land where there is no water.

²Therefore I have gazed upon you in your holy place,
> that I might behold your power and your glory.

³For your steadfast love is better than life itself;
> my lips shall give you praise.

⁴So will I bless you as long as I live
> and lift up my hands in your name.

⁵My spirit is content, as with the richest of foods,
> and my mouth praises you with joyful lips,

⁶when I remember you upon my bed,
> and meditate on you in the night watches.

⁷For you have been my helper,
> and under the shadow of your wings I will rejoice.

⁸My whole being clings to you;
> your right hand holds me fast.

Song
You may sing or pray a song of your choosing, found in the
"Hymns and Songs" section (page 215).

Word
You may want to choose a scripture passage from the
"Praying through the Year" section of this book or from the
"Topical Scripture Suggestions" at the back of this book
(page 209).

Gospel Canticle: Luke 1:68-79
Blessed are you, Lord, the God of Israel,
you have come to your people and set them free.
You have raised up for us a mighty Savior,
born of the house of your servant David.
Through your holy prophets,
     you promised of old to save us from our enemies,
     from the hands of all who hate us,
     to show mercy to our forebears,
     and to remember your holy covenant.
This was the oath you swore to our father Abraham:
     to set us free from the hands of our enemies,
     free to worship you without fear,
     holy and righteous before you, all the days of our life.
And you, child, shall be called the prophet of the Most High,
for you will go before the Lord to prepare the way,
to give God's people knowledge of salvation
by the forgiveness of their sins.
In the tender compassion of our God,
the dawn from on high shall break upon us,
to shine on those who dwell in darkness
and the shadow of death,
and to guide our feet into the way of peace.

Prayers

Below are various prayers that may help you as you begin your day.

I give thanks to you, heavenly Father, through Jesus Christ your dear Son, that you have protected me through the night from all harm and danger. I ask that you would also protect me today from sin and all evil, so that my life and actions may please you. Into your hands I commend myself: my body, my soul, and all that is mine. Let your holy angels be with me, so that the wicked foe may have no power over me. Amen.[49]

Eternal God, my heart this day is filled with fear. Shadows seem to cloud each hour. The path ahead appears filled with problems and threats. Deliver me from senseless worry and protect me in genuine danger. Teach me to trust in your unending love. Let me walk in confidence and strength as your child by faith, following after Jesus Christ, my Savior and Lord. Amen.

Eternal God, walk with me this day, for the problems that I face are complex. The best course of action will not always be clear; the right thing to do is sometimes hard to determine and the struggles I confront are difficult. Assure me of your forgiving love and your steadfast care, that I may face each day with confidence that you will never abandon me. Hear me now, I pray, through Jesus Christ my Savior. Amen.

You may pray the Lord's Prayer, printed on page 240.

Blessing

As you continue into your day, mark your forehead with water in the sign of the cross while saying the following words. In doing this, may you be reminded that through your baptism, you are God's beloved.

Almighty God, the Father, + the Son, and the Holy Spirit, bless and preserve me. Amen.

EVENING PRAYER

Opening
Jesus Christ is the light of the world, the light no darkness can overcome.

Psalmody
You may read Psalm 121 (below) or one of your choosing found in the "Selected Psalms" section (page 191).

¹I lift up my eyes to the hills;
  from where is my help to come?
²My help comes from the Lord,
  the maker of heaven and earth.
³The Lord will not let your foot be moved
  nor will the one who watches over you fall asleep.
⁴Behold, the keeper of Israel
  will neither slumber nor sleep;
⁵the Lord watches over you;
  the Lord is your shade at your right hand;
⁶the sun will not strike you by day,
  nor the moon by night.
⁷The Lord will preserve you from all evil
  and will keep your life.
⁸The Lord will watch over your going out and your coming in,
  from this time forth forevermore.

Song
You may sing or pray a song of your choosing found in the
"Hymns and Songs" section (page 215).

Word
One or more scripture passages may be read, followed by
silence for reflection. The reflection may conclude with
the following:

> Jesus said, "I am the light of the world.
> Whoever follows me will never walk in darkness."

Gospel Canticle: Luke 1:46-55
The gospel canticle for evening, the song of Mary, may
be prayed.

My soul proclaims the greatness of the Lord,
my spirit rejoices in God my Savior,
for you, Lord, have looked with favor on your lowly servant.
From this day all generations will call me blessed:
> you, the Almighty, have done great things for me
> and holy is your name.
> You have mercy on those who fear you,
> from generation to generation.
You have shown strength with your arm
and scattered the proud in their conceit,
casting down the mighty from their thrones
and lifting up the lowly.
You have filled the hungry with good things
and sent the rich away empty.
You have come to the aid of your servant Israel,
to remember the promise of mercy,
the promise made to our forebears,
to Abraham and his children forever.

Prayers

In peace, I pray to you, O Lord. I thank you for the blessings of this day and ask your strength to guide me through the difficult moments, and I bring before you the world you so love.

Especially I pray

for the peace from above and our salvation . . .

for the peace of the whole world . . .

for peace between nations . . .

for peace between cellmates and others who are incarcerated . . .

for peace for my own soul . . .

Other prayers may be added.

I pray to you, O Lord, for others in my life. May the love you have revealed in Jesus Christ comfort, renew, and empower them.

Especially I pray

for those who serve as public servants, for the government, and for those called to protect us . . .

for the president of the United States and all who lead . . .

for those who serve as correctional officers . . .

for those who are incarcerated with me . . .

for those who work to bring peace, justice, healing, and protection in this and every place . . .

for friends and family near and far who support me . . .

Other prayers may be added.

I pray to you, O Lord, for all who are in any need. As you care for all your children, help me to be an instrument of your peace, justice, and healing.

Especially I pray

> for deliverance in times of affliction, danger, and need ...
>
> for those who have been hurt by my actions or who have
> hurt me ...
>
> for those who are sick and suffering ...
>
> for those who are in prison or held captive ...
>
> and for all who await from the Lord great and abundant
> mercy ...

*Other intercessions may be added. A time of silence may
follow, then conclude your prayers with the following:*

Giving thanks for all who have gone before us and are at rest,
rejoicing in the communion of all the saints, I commend myself
and my whole life to you, O Lord. Amen.

*One or more of the following or other appropriate prayers
may be prayed.*

O God, from whom come all holy desires, all good counsels,
and all just works: give to your servants that peace which the
world cannot give, that our hearts may be set to obey your
commandments; and also that we, being defended from the
fear of our enemies, may live in peace and quietness; through
Jesus Christ our Savior, who lives and reigns with you and the
Holy Spirit, God forever. Amen.[50]

I give thanks to you, heavenly Father, through Jesus Christ
your dear Son, that you have graciously protected me today.
I ask you to forgive me all my sins, where I have done wrong,
and graciously to protect me tonight. Into your hands I
commend myself: my body, my soul, and all that is mine. Let
your holy angels be with me, so that the wicked foe may have
no power over me. Amen.[51]

God of justice and mercy, your Son declared release to the captives as a sign of God's reign and promised paradise to the repentant thief on the cross. Give strength and perseverance to me and my family and friends. Make known to us the gracious power of forgiveness through your Son's death and resurrection, that we may support each other throughout this time of separation; and sustain us with the promise of Jesus Christ, through whom all things are made new, and in whose name, I pray. Amen.

You may pray the Lord's Prayer, printed on page 240.

Blessing
The sign of the cross may be made in remembrance of the gift of baptism.

Almighty God, the Father, the + Son, and the Holy Spirit, bless and preserve me. Amen.

NIGHT PRAYER

Opening
Almighty God grant me a quiet night and rest and peace at the last. Amen.

By day, O God, you grant your steadfast love, and at night your song is with me, a prayer to the God of my life.

Night Hymn
All Praise to Thee, My God, This Night

> All praise to thee, my God, this night
> for all the blessings of the light.
> Keep me, oh, keep me, King of kings,
> beneath thine own almighty wings.

Confession
Holy and gracious God, I confess that I have sinned against you this day. Some of my sin I know—the thoughts and words and actions of which I am ashamed—but some is known only to you. In the name of Jesus Christ, I ask forgiveness. Deliver and restore me, that I may rest in peace.

Silence may be kept for self-examination.

Praise to you, O God, for by your mercy I am united with Jesus Christ and in him I am forgiven. May I rest now in the peace of Christ and rise in the morning to serve. Amen.

Psalmody
One or more psalms (such as 4, 34, 91, 130, 139) may be prayed. Each may be followed by a time of silence.

Word

One of the following or another brief scripture passage may be read.

Do not worry, saying, "What will we eat?" or "What will we drink?" or "What will we wear?" Indeed your heavenly Father knows that you need all these things. But strive first for the dominion and the righteousness of God, and all these things will be given to you as well. So do not worry about tomorrow. *(Matthew 6:31-34)*

Come to me, all you that are weary and are carrying heavy burdens, and I will give you rest. Take my yoke upon you, and learn from me; for I am gentle and humble in heart, and you will find rest for your souls. For my yoke is easy, and my burden is light. *(Matthew 11:28-30)*

I am convinced that neither death, nor life, nor angels, nor rulers, nor things present, nor things to come, nor powers, nor height, nor depth, nor anything else in all creation, will be able to separate us from the love of God in Christ Jesus our Lord. *(Romans 8:38-39)*

Humble yourselves under God's mighty hand, so that God may exalt you in due time. Cast all your anxiety on the one who cares for you. Discipline yourselves, keep alert. Like a roaring lion, your adversary the devil prowls around, looking for someone to devour. Resist the devil, steadfast in your faith. *(1 Peter 5:6-9a)*

Silence for reflection and meditation may follow. The silence may conclude:
Into your hands, O Lord, I commend my spirit.
You have redeemed me, O Lord, God of truth.

Into your hands I commend my spirit.
Glory to the Father, and to the Son, and to the Holy Spirit.
Into your hands I commend my spirit.

Gospel Canticle: Luke 2:29-32
Guide us waking, O Lord, and guard us sleeping;
    that awake we may watch with Christ
    and asleep we may rest in peace.
Now, Lord, you let your servant go in peace:
your word has been fulfilled.
My own eyes have seen the salvation
which you have prepared in the sight of every people:
a light to reveal you to the nations
and the glory of your people Israel.
Guide us waking, O Lord, and guard us sleeping:
    that awake we may watch with Christ
    and asleep we may rest in peace.

Prayers
Hear my prayer, O Lord; listen to my cry. Keep me as the
apple of your eye; hide me in the shadow of your wings. In
righteousness, I shall see you; when I awake, your presence
will give me joy.

*One or more of the following or other appropriate prayers
may be prayed.*

Be present, merciful God, and protect me through the hours
of this night, so that I who am wearied by the changes and
chances of life may find my rest in you, through Jesus Christ
my Lord. Amen.

Keep watch, dear Lord, with those who work or watch or weep
this night, and give your angels charge over those who sleep.

Tend the sick, give rest to the weary, bless the dying, soothe the suffering, comfort the afflicted, shield the joyous; and all for your love's sake. Amen.[52]

Gracious God, I give you thanks for the day, especially for the good I was permitted to give and to receive; the day is now past and I commit it to you. I entrust to you the night; I rest securely, for you are my help, and you neither slumber nor sleep; through Jesus Christ my Lord. Amen.[53]

Almighty God, do not let me sink into the depths of depression and sorrow. Give me a glimpse of hope and grant me the strength to seek help. You know that I live in fear and dread. Sometimes I do not even know if I have the courage to face tomorrow. Rescue me through your Spirit. Motivate me to seek help, guidance, and comfort from others, so that I may continue with renewed hope, trusting in your mercy and love. Hear me, I pray, through Jesus Christ my Savior. Amen.

God of peace, the hours are long, the days are hard, life is complex, and fears and anxieties are real. Enable me to lay in your hands the day that is past—the good I have been permitted to do, but also my worries and feelings of uncertainty. As I take a deep breath of gratitude for your constant mercy and love, allow me to sleep in peace, trusting in your unfailing care. Let my sleep be a confession of confidence in your love, which you have shown in Jesus Christ my Savior. Amen.

Lord,
it is night.
The night is for stillness.
Let us be still in the presence of God.
It is night after a long day.

What has been done has been done;
what has not been done has not been done;
let it be.
The night is dark.
Let our fears of the darkness of the world and of our own lives
rest in you.
The night is quiet.
Let the quietness of your peace enfold us,
all dear to us,
and all who have no peace.
The night heralds the dawn.
Let us look expectantly to a new day,
new joys,
new possibilities.
In your name we pray.
Amen.[54]

You may pray the Lord's Prayer, printed on page 240.

Blessing
Now in peace I will lie down and sleep; you alone, O God, make
me secure. Thanks be to God.

PRAYING THROUGH THE DAY

"The LORD grants lovingkindness in the daytime; in the night season the LORD's song is with me, a prayer to the God of my life." (Psalm 42:8).

Probably the biggest challenge in the Bible besides the call to love our enemies is St. Paul's advice to the earliest Christians to "pray without ceasing" (1 Thessalonians 5:17). We Christians have struggled to figure out how to do that ever since. The church as a whole certainly "prays without ceasing" because someone somewhere in the global church is praying at any given time.

But maybe the challenge for us as individual Christians really is what it says—that it is possible by the power of the Holy Spirit for us to draw closer to God in prayer and to entrust every moment of our lives to God. Picture a steady, relentless, constant stream of love, mercy, grace, and hope coming toward each of us. Through prayer, we can actually tap into the power and presence of God, the creator of the universe, at any time—day or night.

How might life be different if we lived in that cosmic truth no matter our circumstances? And how might we adjust the dial of our lives to tune in to that steady stream of God's presence?

The suggestions that follow are only that—suggestions. There is no magic formula for tuning in to God's channel. These are some techniques that have worked for some Christians over the centuries—they've stood the test of time. They are offered here to spark your own imagination and creativity in prayer.

At the Start of the Day

This series of prayers can be used in various ways. You could pray them all in one sitting, dedicating time to each step. That could be two to three minutes for each step for a twenty-minute period of prayer, or ten minutes for each step for an hour of prayer. Or you could try using one of these as your focus each morning, rotating through them over the course of a week.

· First, put yourself into a prayerful frame of mind with a Bible reading, listening for God's word of invitation and challenge for this prayer time. You might use the readings in this book. Look for one verse that will be your theme or mantra for the day, something that you can recall throughout the day. Meditate on it, perhaps even memorize it, or write it where you will see it frequently. Or make up a tune for it and sing it.

· Second, identify five things that you are thankful for, or five dimensions of one thing that you are thankful for. Praise God for these gifts.

· Third, ask for guidance for the day ahead, bringing to mind the things that are troubling you or challenging you, your hopes for the day, your worries for the day ahead. Lift them all to God in prayer.

· Fourth, name before God the people that you want to pray for, one by one: family and friends, those who need healing, those seeking guidance, individuals that you will encounter this day, people who trouble you or that you're having a hard time dealing with. Entrust each one of them to God's care for this day.

- Fifth, stop talking at God and sit in silence for a period of time, seeking to listen to the prompting of the Spirit in your heart and mind. Listen for God's guidance.

- Sixth, invite God to accompany you on the day's journey, and ask the Holy Spirit to remind you of God's presence, power, and guidance in all that you do throughout the day ahead.

- Finish your time of prayer with the confident assurance that "surely the LORD is in this place" (Genesis 28:16).

Throughout the Day
Prayer throughout the activities of the day can be as quick and as intimate as breathing. Anne Lamott says that most of our prayers are just "Help!," "Thanks," or "Wow!"[55] So a quick, "Help me, Jesus!" can provide immediate strength in any challenge.

Brother Lawrence, a French soldier from the seventeenth century who became a monk, looked for God in everything he did, doing what became known as "the practice of the presence of God." He wrote: "A brief remembrance of God, an act of inner adoration—even though on the run with sword in hand—these prayers, short as they may be, are pleasing to God, and, far from causing those engaged in battle to lose courage in the most dangerous circumstances, fortify it."[56] Later, as a monk, Brother Lawrence found that he could worship God just as much at his job working in the monastery kitchen as in the chapel.

Listening for God takes awareness and patience. Often God speaks through a Bible verse or something we read in a book. Sometimes God speaks through dreams. Frequently we realize that God's message to us comes during a conversation with another Christian. Sometimes the subtle prompts of the Holy Spirit just become clear in our minds as we pray, calling us to reach out to a neighbor—or even an enemy—in support and love, or to take action for restoration and justice, or to work for change in an institution or system.

Keeping a Spiritual Journal through Words, Songs, or Art

Many Christians find that writing a journal helps to keep track of how frequently and powerfully God is active in our lives. We may not always recognize God at work when we are in the midst of a difficult situation. But after we get through that time of trial, when we look back, we can see where God was protecting us and guiding us through the storm. Keeping a prayer journal, either through words or songs or drawings or even doodling, can remind us of all the places and times God has answered our prayers in creative, powerful, unexpected, and sometimes miraculous ways.

At the End of the Day

At the end of each day, take some time to review the day in the presence of God, to shine God's light of love and mercy into the thoughts, feelings, and activities of the day that has ended. When we look prayerfully, we can identify places where God has been active in the ordinary events and encounters of the day. Saint Ignatius of Loyola developed the *Examen*, a six-step prayer practice that brings the day just past into the healing light of Christ and challenges us to identify what God is calling us to do tomorrow.

- First, take a moment to quiet your mind and enter into silence. Invite God's presence into your awareness.

- Second, look back over the day. What did you do today? Who did you encounter today? Review your feelings: What made you glad? mad? bored? thankful? Offer your activities and emotions to God.

- Third, think about where God was present today. When or how were you in sync with God? When did God lead you in unexpected ways?

- Fourth, were there times where you didn't feel God's presence or failed to listen for God's guidance? Do you need to ask forgiveness from God or from someone you encountered today? Is God calling you to do something tomorrow?

- Fifth, give thanks for whatever good has come from this day and receive it as God's gift. Praise God for this love and mercy.

- Finally, entrust the day to God and rest in God's peace.

"Let inward prayer be your last act before you fall asleep and the first act when you awake."[57] The cycle of ceaseless prayer turns again, for God has promised always to be tuned in, to hear our voices, and to respond whenever and however we pray.

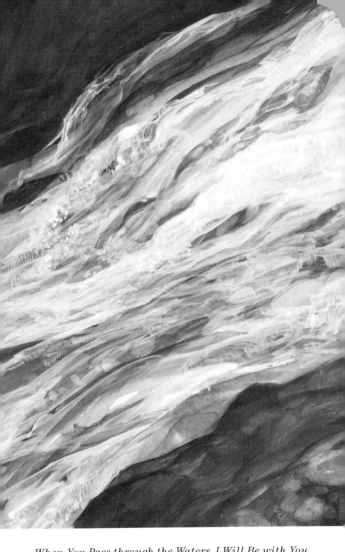

When You Pass through the Waters, I Will Be with You

Do not fear, for I have redeemed you;
I have called you by name,
you are mine.

—Isaiah 43:1

GROUP PRAYERS IN PRISON

AFFIRMATION OF BAPTISM IN VARIOUS CIRCUMSTANCES

How to Use This Section

We are given many names in life: the things people call us and the names we call ourselves. Those names can be uplifting or they can be hurtful and degrading. In our baptism, whether as an infant or an adult, God gives each of us the name "Child of God" and claims us as God's own. It is important to be reminded of that name and what it means to be God's child and to live in God's ways. That is why we affirm, or remember and reclaim, our baptism: to be reminded of who and whose we are. This small service can be done within a worship service or in the community of two or three persons. This service may be led by a chaplain or by any believer.

Gathering

If possible, a bowl of water may be placed in the midst of those who are gathered. If this order takes place in the chapel, the baptismal font may be used as the place of gathering.

Those present may make the sign of the cross, the sign marked at baptism, as the leader begins.

Blessed be the holy Trinity, + one God, the fountain of living water, the rock who gave us birth, our light and our salvation. **Amen.**

The leader may note the occasion for this affirmation. These or similar words may also be used.
Dear friends, we give thanks for the gift of baptism, and we come before God with _name/s_ as *they* make affirmation of *their* baptism into Christ.

Let us pray.
Merciful God, we thank you that you have made us your own by water and the Word in baptism. You have called us to yourself, enlightened us with the gifts of your Spirit, and nourished us in the community of faith. Uphold us and all your servants in the gifts and promises of baptism, and unite the hearts of all whom you have brought to new birth. We ask this in the name of Christ.
Amen.

Reading
One or more scripture passages may be read. Readings may be selected from other sections of this volume, or other appropriate readings may be chosen.

Silence for reflection may follow the reading of scripture. Other forms of reflection may also follow, such as brief comment by the leader, personal witness by one who is making an affirmation of baptism, or guided conversation among those present.

A hymn may be sung.

Profession of Faith
*The leader addresses those making affirmation of
their baptism.*

I ask you to profess your faith in Christ Jesus, reject sin, and
confess the faith of the church.

Do you renounce the devil and all the forces that defy God?
Response: I renounce them.

Do you renounce the powers of this world that rebel against God?
Response: I renounce them.

Do you renounce the ways of sin that draw you from God?
Response: I renounce them.

Do you believe in God the Father?
**I believe in God, the Father almighty,
  creator of heaven and earth.**

Do you believe in Jesus Christ, the Son of God?
**I believe in Jesus Christ, God's only Son, our Lord,
  who was conceived by the Holy Spirit,
  born of the virgin Mary,
  suffered under Pontius Pilate,
  was crucified, died, and was buried;
  he descended to the dead.
  On the third day he rose again;
  he ascended into heaven,
  he is seated at the right hand of the Father,
  and he will come to judge the living and the dead.**

Do you believe in God the Holy Spirit?
I believe in the Holy Spirit,
the holy catholic church,
the communion of saints,
the forgiveness of sins,
the resurrection of the body,
and the life everlasting.

Affirmation
The leader addresses those who are making affirmation of their baptism.

You have made profession of your faith. Do you intend to
continue in the covenant God made with you in holy baptism:
  to live among God's faithful people,
  to hear the word of God and share in the Lord's supper,
  to proclaim the good news of God in Christ
    through word and deed,
  to serve all people, following the example of Jesus,
  and to strive for justice and peace in all the earth?
Response: I do, and I ask God to help and guide me.

The leader may address others who are present.
People of God, do you promise to support *name/s* and pray for
them in *their* life in Christ?
We do, and we ask God to help and guide us.

The leader prays for God's blessing.
Let us pray.

We give you thanks, O God, that through water and the Holy
Spirit you give us new birth, cleanse us from sin, and raise us
to eternal life.

*The following words of blessing may be repeated for each
person. The leader may lay both hands on the head of the
person and say:*

Stir up in name the gift of your Holy Spirit: the spirit of
wisdom and understanding, the spirit of counsel and might,
the spirit of knowledge and the fear of the Lord, the spirit of
joy in your presence, both now and forever. Amen.

The leader continues.

Name/s , we rejoice with you in the life of baptism. Together we
will give thanks and praise to God and proclaim the good news
to all the world.

*A hymn, song, or psalm may be sung and may be
accompanied by a reminder of baptism.*

Prayers
You may pray the Lord's Prayer, printed on page 240.

Blessing
The order concludes with this or another suitable blessing.

Almighty God, who gives us a new birth by water and the Holy
Spirit and forgives us all our sins, strengthen us in all goodness
and by the power of the Holy Spirit keep us in eternal life,
through Jesus Christ our Lord. Amen.

A LITURGY OF HEALING AND HOPE

How to Use This Section
This prayer service is for a group of people to pray together as they seek healing in some form:

- from drug or alcohol addiction;
- from sexual abuse or domestic violence;
- from discrimination based on their ethnicity, sexual orientation, or gender identity;
- from serious illnesses;
- from grief and depression, especially during holidays
- from any situation that calls for God's healing and restoration of hope.

The words that are spoken by a leader(s) are in regular type. Words spoken by all are in boldface type.

Gathering
The Lord be with you.
And also with you.
Let us pray.

This is another day, O Lord. I know not what it will bring forth, but make me ready, Lord, for whatever it may be. If I am to stand up, help me to stand bravely. If I am to sit still, help me to sit quietly. If I am to lie low, help me to do it patiently. And if I am to do nothing, let me do it gallantly. Make these words more than words and give me the Spirit of Jesus. Amen.[58]

Isaiah 43:1-3, 5
But now thus says the LORD, he who created you, O Jacob, he who formed you, O Israel: Do not fear, for I have redeemed you; I have called you by name, you are mine. When you pass

through the waters, I will be with you; and through the rivers, they shall not overwhelm you; when you walk through fire you shall not be burned, and the flame shall not consume you. For I am the LORD your God, the Holy One of Israel, your Savior. . . . Do not fear, for I am with you; I will bring your offspring from the east, and from the west I will gather you.

Silence

Psalm 86:1-12 *(read responsively by half verse)*
¹Bow down your ear, O LORD, and answer me,
 for I am poor and in misery.
²Keep watch over my life, for I am faithful;
 save your servant who trusts in you.
³Be merciful to me, O LORD, for you are my God;
 I call upon you all the day long.
⁴Gladden the soul of your servant,
 for to you, O Lord, I lift up my soul.
⁵For you, O Lord, are good and forgiving,
 and abundant in mercy toward all who call upon you.
⁶Give ear, O LORD, to my prayer,
 and attend to the voice of my supplications.
⁷In the time of my trouble I will call upon you,
 for you will answer me.
⁸Among the gods there is none like you, O Lord,
 nor anything like your works.
⁹All the nations you have made
 will come and worship you, O Lord,
 and glorify your name.
¹⁰For you are great; you do wondrous things;
 and you alone are God.
¹¹Teach me your way, O LORD, and I will walk in your truth;
 give me an undivided heart to revere your name.

[12]I will thank you, O Lord my God, with all my heart,
and glorify your name forevermore.

Silence

Song
There's a Wideness in God's Mercy (stanza 1)

> There's a wideness in God's mercy,
> like the wideness of the sea;
> there's a kindness in God's justice
> which is more than liberty.
> There is no place where earth's sorrows
> are more felt than up in heav'n.
> There is no place where earth's failings
> have such kindly judgment giv'n.

A Litany of Healing and Hope[59]
I: When will help come?

We are haunted and afraid by what we cannot understand.
When will our help come, O God?

We are tired, aching, and empty.
When will our help come, O God?

Our bodies betray our past, bearing so many wounds not
yet healed.
When will our help come, O God?

We are weary of the trauma relived and repeated in our lives,
our relationships, and our bodies.
When will our help come, O God?

II. Be present

We are lost and alone in our grief.
Be present to us in our anguish, O God.

Our children do not know us; we do not know ourselves.
Be present to us in our anguish, O God.

Our relationships suffer; too many people use us and sin against us.
Be present to us in our anguish, O God.

We bear the pain of our trauma alone; our substances have become our refuge.
Be present to us in our anguish, O God.

III. Heal us

In our pain, we have lost our connection to you and to our true selves.
Heal us, most merciful God.

The burden of our guilt weighs on our hearts and minds.
Heal us, most merciful God.

We wrestle with the consequences of our choices and long for new beginnings.
Heal us, most merciful God.

We struggle to find peace and to trust in your mercy.
Heal us, most merciful God.

IV: Make us whole

Help us heal our broken bodies and broken spirits.
God of great compassion, make us whole again.

Teach us to love ourselves and our bodies, and to love one
another as children of God.
God of great compassion, make us whole again.

Grant us the courage to breathe in the truth of your grace and
to turn our grief into wonder.
God of great compassion, make us whole again.

Renew us by your Holy Spirit that we may become the people
you have made us to be.
Amen.

Song
There's a Wideness in God's Mercy (stanza 2)

> There is welcome for the sinner,
> and a promised grace made good;
> there is mercy with the Savior;
> there is healing in his blood.
> There is grace enough for thousands
> of new worlds as great as this;
> there is room for fresh creations
> in that upper home of bliss.

Matthew 11:28-30
Come to me, all you that are weary and are carrying heavy
burdens, and I will give you rest. Take my yoke upon you,
and learn from me; for I am gentle and humble in heart, and

you will find rest for your souls. For my yoke is easy, and my burden is light.

Closing Prayer

Gracious and loving God, we come before you today, broken yet being healed through your love. Be present with us always, even when we only feel your absence. Give us the courage to stand in the shadow of the cross of your beloved Son and see your love laid open for us in that sacrifice. Give us the strength to mourn what has been lost and to bear the traumas of our past, knowing that you are with us in the present. Meet us in our brokenness and remind us that we are whole, and we are yours. Fill us with the light and hope to see ourselves—our bodies, minds, and spirits—as you see us: beloved children of the living God. Amen.

A LITANY FOR RECONCILIATION AND WELCOME[60]

How to Use This Section

This prayer service is a blessing upon those who have just left prison. It allows the challenges of this transition to be named and claimed by both those returning and those in the community receiving them back. It may be used within a worship service, in a Bible study, or in a support group or other gathering as appropriate. The leader portions are spoken by those who are returning to the community; the people are those welcoming them back. If possible, place a cross in the worship space and have paper and pencils/pens available for writing.

The words that are spoken by a leader(s) are in regular type. Words spoken by all are in boldface type.

Welcome
We take this time to acknowledge the work of reunion that we are doing every day. We understand that this is hard work, but we will not step away from it.

Silence for reflection. A song may be sung.

During this time, you will hear the leaders recite a litany that calls us to think about how we may have sinned against others. You are invited to write down your own sins on cards, and toward the end of the service, they will be placed at the foot of the cross.

Pause for reflection and to allow time for writing.

Let us remember that healing requires fully understanding the wounds that have been caused.
For we all have caused wounds.

Let us not try to rush the healing of a wound that may be in need of deep attention and much care.
For we all need and desire healing.

Let us not be defensive when we are presented with the pain we have caused others.
For we all desire to be heard and understood.

Let us not neglect our relationships by valuing material possessions over human lives.
For we all are made in the image of God and each of us is a treasure in a clay jar.

Let us acknowledge that life is messy, that reunions may be painful, and that life within community may never be easy. **For we cannot clean up the messes or ease the pains that we do not admit we have caused.**

Pause for reflection

We understand, firsthand, that the criminal justice system is neither blind nor just, and we carry the scars of those wounds.

Let us grieve violations of personal and social trust.

Let us mourn our losses, especially the losses of black, brown, and indigenous men, women, and children, those disproportionately harmed by the problems within the criminal justice system.

Let us learn about, imagine, and advocate for alternatives to incarceration, that the criminal justice system might better serve God's desire for human flourishing.

Lord, in your mercy, show us how we have treated others unjustly. We ask forgiveness for the times when we have witnessed injustices and remained silent. Fill us with the Holy Spirit and a passion for righteousness.

Listen to Paul's words of comfort and know that the love of Christ pushes through all that distances us from each other and from God, moving those things beyond the cross.

While a leader gathers the cards and moves them to the foot of the cross, another leader continues with the scripture reading.

2 Corinthians 5:15-21

[Christ] died for all, so that those who live might live no longer for themselves, but for him who died and was raised for them. From now on, therefore, we regard no one from a human point of view; even though we once knew Christ from a human point of view, we know him no longer in that way. So if anyone is in Christ, there is a new creation: everything old has passed away; see, everything has become new! All this is from God, who reconciled us to himself through Christ, and has given us the ministry of reconciliation; that is, in Christ God was reconciling the world to himself, not counting their trespasses against them, and entrusting the message of reconciliation to us. So we are ambassadors for Christ, since God is making his appeal through us; we entreat you on behalf of Christ, be reconciled to God. For our sake he made him to be sin who knew no sin, so that in him we might become the righteousness of God.

Prayer for Healing and Hope

Let us pray with our entire being:

God of compassion, help us to forgive the crimes that have been committed in our community. Help us to welcome and support our siblings who have returned to us. Amid all that has troubled our community and challenged our families and our faith, it is our hearts' desire to be healed. Just as we desire to be healed, we desire the scales of justice to balance and the grace of God to prevail. We want love to be released and healing to come to our community. Amen.

Dismissal

Go and share God's love and hope.
Thanks be to God!

COMMENDATION OF THE DYING[61]

How to Use This Section
For centuries Christians have kept vigil and prayed with
people who are dying, commending them to God. This service
offers that opportunity. Everyone deserves to know they are
loved in their living and in their dying, and everyone deserves
to know they are not alone, especially at the time of death.
This service provides an opportunity for you to offer prayer
with someone who is dying. This service may be led by a
chaplain or by any believer.

Scripture Readings
*One or more of the following can be read with the dying
person. Or the dying person's favorite text may be chosen.*

The Lord is my light and my salvation; whom then shall I fear?
(Psalm 27:1)

Into your hands I commend my spirit, for you have redeemed
me, O Lord, God of truth. (Psalm 31:5)

Jesus said, "Come, you that are blessed by my Father, inherit
the kingdom prepared for you from the foundation of the
world." (Matthew 25:34)

Jesus said, "Today you will be with me in Paradise."
(Luke 23:43)

God so loved the world that he gave his only Son, so that
everyone who believes in him may not perish but may have
eternal life. (John 3:16)

Whether we live or whether we die, we are the Lord's.
(Romans 14:8)

Greeting and Prayer
We are gathered for prayer to commend _name_ to God, who is
faithful and compassionate.

Let us pray. Holy God, whose peace surpasses all
understanding, we pray that you will free _name_ from all
earthly cares, release _name_ from pain, and grant that _name_
may come to dwell with all your saints in everlasting glory, for
the sake of Jesus Christ, our Savior and Lord. Amen.

Litany
Let us pray for _name_. [saying, "Deliver your servant."]

Holy God, creator of heaven and earth,
deliver your servant.
Holy and Mighty, redeemer of the world,
deliver your servant.
Holy and Immortal, giver of grace,
deliver your servant.
Holy, blessed, and glorious Trinity, one God,
deliver your servant.

By your holy birth among us,
deliver your servant.
By your cross and passion,
deliver your servant.
By your precious death and burial,
deliver your servant.
By your glorious resurrection and ascension,
deliver your servant.

By the coming of your Holy Spirit,
deliver your servant.

From all evil, all sin, and all trials,
deliver your servant.
From eternal death,
deliver your servant.
By the forgiveness of all _name_'s sins,
deliver your servant.
Into a place of refreshment at your heavenly banquet,
deliver your servant.
Into joy and gladness with your saints in light,
deliver your servant.

The leader then says,
Lord, have mercy. Christ, have mercy. Lord, have mercy. **Amen.**

You may pray the Lord's Prayer, printed on page 240.

Commendation
Let us commend _name_ to the mercy of God.

Name, child of God, go forth in the name of God the Father
Almighty who created you; in the name of Jesus Christ, the
Son of the living God, who redeemed you; in the name of the
Holy Spirit who was poured out upon you. May you rest in
peace and dwell forever in the paradise of God. **Amen.**

When death seems near, the leader continues,
Into your hands, O merciful Savior, we commend your servant
name. Acknowledge, we humbly ask you, a sheep of your
own fold, a lamb of your own flock, a sinner of your own
redeeming. Receive _name_ into the arms of your mercy, into

the blessed rest of everlasting peace, and into the glorious company of the saints in light. **Amen.**

Song
A song may be sung. See "Hymns and Songs" section (page 215).

O Lord, support us all the day long of this troubled life, until the shadows lengthen, and the evening comes, and the busy world is hushed, the fever of life is over, and our work is done. Then, in your mercy, grant us a safe lodging, and a holy rest, and peace at the last; through Jesus Christ our Lord. **Amen.**

Prayers may be included for those who grieve, and all present may be invited to offer their own prayers.

Blessing
May _name_ and all the faithful departed, through the mercy of God, rest in peace. **Amen.**

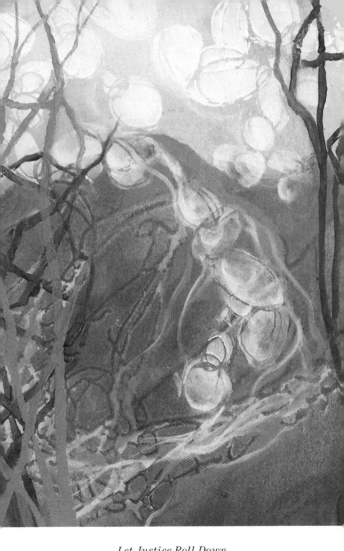

Let Justice Roll Down

*What does the LORD require of you
but to do justice, and to love kindness,
and to walk humbly with your God?*

—*Micah 6:8*

ADDITIONAL
WAYS TO PRAY

GROUP AND INDIVIDUAL BIBLE STUDY

The women's Bible study at the Alexandria Jail was not going particularly well. The Bible study leaders from the nearby seminary over-eagerly shared their knowledge of the scripture passage. Jesus seemed locked in an irrelevant story from long ago and far away. Suddenly, one of the women from inside said, "Jesus did a miracle for me today." She shared how her day and her future had been unexpectedly and miraculously transformed, and she thanked Jesus for his work in her life. As we then all began sharing how God was at work in our lives, Jesus was freed from the text and stood among us, resurrected and powerfully present in that upper room, the law library of the jail. That's the power of Bible study.

As a collection of books written over a wide range of years, the Bible is sometimes confusing. But you don't have to be a pastor or a trained theologian to hear God speaking through the words of Scripture. Martin Luther describes the Bible as "the manger in which Christ lies,"[62] meaning that when we study the Bible prayerfully, Christ will reveal himself to us—often in surprising ways, like how God showed up as Jesus, born in a stable and laid in a manger. The Spirit opens our hearts and minds to hear God's word to the church over the centuries and to encounter God's message to each of us in the moment of prayer. Here are some methods of Bible study for groups or for personal devotion.

Listening for God's Word in Scripture: Lectio Divina

Lectio divina is a formal term that just means reading a piece of scripture slowly, meditatively, and prayerfully. We're not trying to analyze the Bible passage, but instead we use the reading as a doorway into God's presence and as a way to listen for God's guidance. After you select a particular Bible passage for your meditation, lectio divina has four steps:

- Read the passage slowly, concentrating on what it says. Sit quietly with the passage for a few minutes.
- Read the passage again, reflecting on what it might be saying *to you*. What word or phrase jumps out at you? What might God be saying to you about your present situation through this passage?
- Read the passage a third time, this time praying and reflecting on your response to the passage. Does the passage reassure you? Challenge you? Inspire you to try something new? Console you?
- Rest in silence and let the passage that you've just prayed through soak into your soul. Open your heart to the promptings of the Holy Spirit.[63]

How might you pray your own response to the messages of this scripture meditation?

Praying with Eyes Open: Visio Divina

The imagination of artists can reveal the beauty and power of God's infinite creativity. This can be particularly true with artwork inspired by Bible texts, such as the artwork in this book. *Visio divina* means "divine seeing." Meditating on a painting, a photograph, an icon, or even a garden reveals God in a new way. We want to use the art like a mirror that reflects God's image. We can encounter God's love through the talents of the artist.

Here are steps you might use in meditating on a piece of artwork to find God's revelation in it:

- Big picture: As you begin to look at the art, what draws your eye first? What do you see in the image? How do the colors make you feel? What does the image stir up in you?
- As you begin to focus on the details, how does the art begin to reveal and interpret a certain Bible text? How does the image invite you into God's presence?
- Where do you see yourself in the picture? Does the art reveal anything to you about the longings of your heart right now? How might God be speaking to you through this piece of art?
- Rest quietly in the beauty of the art. Let the Spirit of God feed your soul, mind, and heart through the image.

How might you draw your own prayer response to the messages of the art?

Singing God's Word: Audio Divina

As with art, music can offer a new way of encountering God. We might hear God's word in the words of the song and encounter God's creation though the melodies and harmonies of music—either through recorded music that we listen to or through songs and hymns that we sing.

Here are steps you might use in meditating on a piece of music to experience God's revelation through it:

- Listen to the whole piece all the way through. How does the music capture your imagination? What line of text or portion of the melody catches your ear?
- Listen to the piece again. How does the music invite you into God's presence?
- Does the music speak to the longings of your heart right now? Is God speaking to you through this piece of music?
- Rest quietly in the beauty of the music. Let the Spirit of God feed your soul, mind, and heart through the piece.

In Colossians 3:16, the apostle Paul says: "With gratitude in your hearts sing psalms, hymns, and spiritual songs to God." How might you sing your own prayer response to the messages of the music?

Body Prayers

We often use our bodies to help focus our minds in prayer. Sometimes we kneel to pray. We hold up our arms in a prayer posture of openness and receptiveness or fold our hands in prayer. Coordinating our prayers with our breathing in and out can invite the Spirit—God's breath—into our lives in a physical and prayerful way as we inhale and exhale.

Breathe in God's love; breathe out your gratitude.
Breathe in God's forgiveness; breathe out your guilt.
Breathe in God's mercy; breathe out your hope.
Breathe in God's grace; breathe out your joy.
Breathe in God's peace; breathe out your praise.
Breathe in God's promise; breathe out your adoration.
Breathe.

A Dozen Scripture Passages for Group or Individual Bible Study

Genesis 28:10-17 *Jacob's Dream*

Exodus 3 *Moses meets God at the burning bush*
1 Kings 19:1-13 *Elijah meets God on the mountain*
Matthew 14:1-12 *John the Baptist and the death penalty*
Matthew 22:34-39 *Loving God and neighbor*
Mark 4:35-41 *Jesus stills a storm* (also Luke 8:22-25)
Mark 5:1-20 *Jesus heals a chained man*
Luke 4:14-30 *Jesus preaches in the synagogue*
Luke 17:11-19 *The thankful healed leper*
Luke 18:1-8 *Jesus' parable to pray always*
Luke 24:13-35 *Jesus meets his friends after the resurrection*
Acts 16:16-34 *Paul and Silas in prison in Philippi*

SCRIPTURE ARROW PRAYERS[64]

How to Use This Section
Almost any verse of scripture can be transformed into a
quick prayer aimed toward God. These "arrow prayers" can be
used to "pray without ceasing" throughout the day. Below are
some examples.

- I know that you are with me and will keep me wherever I
  go. *(Genesis 28:15)*
- Almighty God, teach me to keep still and let you fight for
  me. *(Exodus 14:14)*
- Make my heart your sanctuary and dwell within me.
  (Exodus 25:8)
- Be a stronghold in times of trouble, O God. I put my trust
  in you. *(Psalm 9:9)*
- O Lord, you are my rock, my fortress, and my deliverer, my
  shield, and my stronghold. *(Psalm 18:1-2)*
- Answer me in the day of trouble, O my God; may your
  name protect me! *(Psalm 20:1)*

- Rock of Ages, be a hiding place for me; preserve me from trouble and surround me with glad cries of deliverance. *(Psalm 32:7)*
- Fight against those who fight against me! Shield me and rise up to help me. *(Psalm 35:1-2)*
- O my God, listen to my cry; do not hold your peace at my tears. *(Psalm 39:12)*
- When I am afraid, I will trust in you, O Most High. *(Psalm 56:2-3)*
- Be merciful to me, O God, be merciful to me, for in you my soul takes refuge. *(Psalm 57:1)*
- O my God, why do you cast me off? Why do you hide your face from me? *(Psalm 88:14)*
- May your name be praised from the rising of the sun to its setting. *(Psalm 113:3)*
- I sing your praise for your steadfast love and your faithfulness. *(Psalm 138:2)*
- Protect me from the violent who have planned my downfall. *(Psalm 140:4)*
- Bring me out of prison, so that I may give thanks to your name. *(Psalm 142:7)*
- I believe; help my unbelief! *(Mark 9:24)*
- Grant me justice against my opponent, O Righteous Judge. *(Luke 18:3)*
- Jesus, remember me when you come into your kingdom. *(Luke 23:42)*
- Jesus, show me the way, teach me your truth, and guide my life. *(John 14:6)*
- Holy Spirit, help me, for I do not know how to pray as I should. *(Romans 8:26)*
- Fill me with all joy and peace in believing, so that I may abound in hope. *(Romans 15:13)*
- Risen One, help me to walk by faith and not by sight. *(2 Corinthians 5:7)*

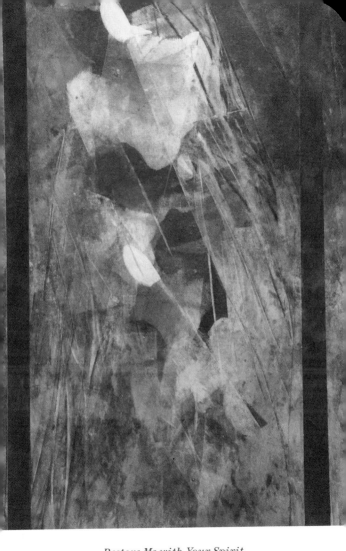

Restore Me with Your Spirit

*Hear my cry, O God, and
listen to my prayer.*

—Psalm 61:1

PRAYING WITH IMPRISONED SAINTS

How to Use This Section

Many Christians have spent days, months, years, or even decades imprisoned. Today many believers honor these Christians imprisoned long ago as saints because of the faith they expressed before, during, and after their incarceration. Here are descriptions of five such imprisoned saints, along with prayers inspired by their lives. Invite these disciples of faith into your cell as prayer companions with you across the centuries.

Joan of Arc, 1412–1431

England and France were at war during the 1400s over the ownership of land that is now part of France. Joan of Arc was a teenage peasant girl who had visions from angels and saints who told her to lead an army against the British. She put on armor and led the French soldiers in a series of victorious battles. But she was betrayed to the English, who imprisoned her and tried her for heresy (believing religious doctrines opposed to the official teaching of the church) and witchcraft, a charge that has been levied at many women who showed extraordinary power over men. One of the primary charges against her was that she dressed as a man, which was a high crime in the fifteenth century. At nineteen years old, she was burned at the stake. A church court absolved her of all charges five years after her death.

Here is a quote from Joan of Arc's trial testimony, when she was asked to tell the court what she had prayed:

Most sweet God, in honor of your holy passion, I beg you, if you love me, to reveal to me how I must respond to these churchmen. As for the dress, I know well the command by which I have taken it; but I do not know in what way I must leave it. May it therefore please you to teach it to me.[65]

Remembering Joan of Arc, we pray:
O God, my shield and defender, I thank you for sending your angels and saints to accompany me throughout my days. Guide me as each day I try to live my beliefs. Be my armor against all harm and evil. Show me how to live my life for you. In Jesus' name I pray. Amen.

William Tyndale, 1494–1536

William Tyndale was a devout Christian theologian and a language expert living in England during the rise of Protestantism. At that time, the king maintained rigid control of all religious matters. The government upheld a church law that required everyone to use the Latin version of the Bible; any biblical translation into English was forbidden. Tyndale produced an excellent English translation of the Bible from its original Greek and Hebrew. For this, he was arrested, jailed for a year, and then executed: strangled at the stake and his body burned. Some of his biblical wording is familiar to us, such as "the salt of the earth," "the spirit is willing but the flesh is weak," and "we live, move, and have our being." Seventy-five years after Tyndale's execution, King James I authorized an English translation of the Bible, and 83 percent of this translation was copied from Tyndale's work.

Here is an excerpt from a letter Tyndale wrote from Vilvorde Prison:

I beg your lordship, and that by the Lord Jesus, that if I am to remain here through the winter, you will request the commissary to have the kindness to send me . . . a warmer cap; for I suffer greatly from cold in the head . . . which is much increased in this cell.... And I ask to be allowed to have a lamp in the evening; it is indeed wearisome sitting alone in the dark.... If any decision has been taken concerning me [i.e. execution], to be carried out before winter, I will be patient, abiding the will of God, to the glory of the grace of my Lord Jesus Christ: whose Spirit (I pray) may ever direct your heart.[66]

Remembering William Tyndale, we pray:
O God, comforter and companion, I thank you for speaking to me through the Scriptures in my own language. I pray that your good news will open up my heart to you and to my neighbors, that I may find my freedom in you. In Jesus' name I pray. Amen.

Anne Hutchinson, 1592-1643

In 1634 Anne Hutchinson moved from England and settled with her husband and children in colonial Boston. She worked as a midwife and healer and became famous as a teacher of the faith. She gathered women into her home to discuss various passages from the Bible, including some texts from recent local sermons. While pregnant with her fifteenth child, she was arrested and accused of stirring up religious controversy in the colony by publicly disagreeing with some of the clergy's sermons when she met with the women, and improperly functioning as a teacher of men because some men had attended her sessions. Judged a heretic, she was imprisoned during the winter of 1637 and then exiled to Rhode Island. Later settled in what became New York City, she and her children were killed by Siwanoy Indians during a local conflict. Some of her accusers considered her prior delivery of a deformed baby and this violent death to be signs of God's judgment on her religious convictions.

Here is an excerpt from Anne Hutchinson's trial:

Now if you do condemn me for speaking what in my conscience I know to be truth, I must commit myself unto the Lord.... You have power over my body, but the Lord Jesus hath power over my body and soul.[67]

Remembering Anne Hutchinson, we pray:
O God, Word of Life, I bless you for all the women who have spoken of Christ to their neighbors. In your mercy, sustain all abused women, whether here or around the globe, and comfort those who experience sexism and jealousy. Keep me confident of your presence, no matter where I am forced to live, for I know that my life is in you. In Jesus' name I pray. Amen.

Dietrich Bonhoeffer, 1906–1945
Dietrich Bonhoeffer became a Lutheran pastor and theologian during the rise of Hitler's Nazi regime in Germany. Although he taught for a while at Union Theological Seminary in New York City, he returned to Germany, believing that God was calling him to witness against the anti-Semitism and nationalism of the Nazi party. He became a leader in the Confessing Church, an underground Christian group that worked to oppose the Nazis. He joined in an unsuccessful plot to assassinate Hitler. Bonhoeffer admitted his part in the conspiracy, praying that God would judge such an action ethical. After two years in prison, Bonhoeffer was hanged by the Nazi regime just two weeks before the Allies liberated the prison. The collection of his *Letters and Papers from Prison* became a best-seller. He is most famous for explaining "the cost of discipleship": what it means and what it costs to be a follower of Jesus Christ.

Here is an excerpt from Dietrich Bonhoeffer's writing:

The cross is laid on every Christian.... The cross is not the terrible end of a pious happy life. Instead, it stands at the beginning of community with Jesus Christ.... Because Jesus' every command calls us to die with all our wishes and desires, and because we cannot want our own death, therefore Jesus Christ in his word has to be our death and our life. The call to follow Jesus, baptism in the name of Jesus Christ, is death and life.[68]

Remembering Dietrich Bonhoeffer, we pray:
O God, I thank you for the cost Jesus paid for my salvation. Forgive all my sins and offenses, no matter how the world judges me. Throughout my life and death, protect me by the cross of Christ, and give me companions in discipleship, no matter where I live. In Jesus' name I pray. Amen.

Martin Luther King Jr., 1929–1968
Martin Luther King Jr. was the minister of an American Baptist church in Montgomery, Alabama, who became a leader in the African American civil rights movement. He had studied the history of nonviolent resistance to unjust laws and dedicated his life to following Jesus. He worked toward fairness for the disenfranchised, equality for people of color, and the alleviation of poverty. Despite much Christian opposition, he argued that Christians have a moral responsibility to break laws that are unjust, and he presented this position in his famous "Letter from Birmingham City Jail," written while he was incarcerated in 1963. On April 4, 1968, he was assassinated in Memphis, where he was planning a nonviolent demonstration in support of persons living in poverty.

Here is an excerpt from one of his sermons:

God is at work in his universe. He is not outside the world looking on with a sort of cold indifference. Here on all the roads of life, he is striving in our striving. Like an ever-loving Father, he is working through history for the salvation of his children. As we struggle to defeat the forces of evil, the God of the universe struggles with us. Evil dies on the seashore, not merely because of man's endless struggle against it, but because of God's power to defeat it.[69]

Remembering Martin Luther King Jr., we pray:
O God of the universe, I praise you for accompanying your people through all their miseries. Throughout history you have attacked the power of evil. Be at work in me. Strengthen my trust in your care. Show me which laws call for my obedience, and which laws call for nonviolent resistance. Guide this nation in your will and your way. In Jesus' name I pray. Amen.

Let My Prayer Rise before You

*Let your lovingkindness,
O Lord, be upon us, even as we
place our hope in you.*

—Psalm 33:22

SCRIPTURE AND SONG

SELECTED PSALMS

Psalm 4

[1]Answer me when I call, O God, defender of my cause;
   you set me free when I was in distress; have mercy on me
   and hear my prayer.
[2]"You mortals, how long will you dishonor my glory;
   how long will you love illusions and seek after lies?"
[3]Know that the Lord does wonders for the faithful;
   The Lord will hear me when I call.
[4]Tremble, then, and do not sin;
   speak to your heart in silence upon your bed.
[5]Offer the appointed sacrifices,
   and put your trust in the Lord.
[6]Many are saying, "Who will show us any good?"
   Let the light of your face shine upon us, O Lord.
[7]You have put gladness in my heart,
   more than when grain and wine abound.
[8]In peace, I will lie down and sleep;
   for you alone, O Lord, make me rest secure.

Psalm 22:1-4, 7-11, 20-21, 25-27

[1]My God, my God, why have you forsaken me?

Why so far from saving me, so far from the words of
my groaning?

[2]My God, I cry out by day, but you do not answer;

by night, but I find no rest.

[3]Yet you are the Holy One,

enthroned on the praises of Israel.

[4]Our ancestors put their trust in you,

they trusted, and you rescued them.

[7]All who see me laugh me to scorn;

they curl their lips; they shake their heads.

[8]"Trust in the LORD; let the LORD deliver;

let God rescue him if God so delights in him."

[9]Yet you are the one who drew me forth from the womb,

and kept me safe on my mother's breast.

[10]I have been entrusted to you ever since I was born;

you were my God when I was still in my mother's womb.

[11]Be not far from me, for trouble is near,

and there is no one to help.

[20]Deliver me from the sword,

my life from the power of the dog.

[21]Save me from the lion's mouth!

From the horns of wild bulls you have rescued me.

[25]From you comes my praise in the great assembly;

I will perform my vows in the sight of those who
fear the LORD.

[26]The poor shall eat and be satisfied.

Let those who seek the LORD give praise!

May your hearts live forever!

[27]All the ends of the earth shall remember and turn
to the LORD;

all the families of nations shall bow before God.

Psalm 23

[1]The LORD is my shepherd;
    I shall not be in want.
[2]The LORD makes me lie down in green pastures
    and leads me beside still waters.
[3]You restore my soul, O LORD,
    and guide me along right pathways for your name's sake.
[4]Though I walk through the valley of the shadow of death, I
    shall fear no evil;
    for you are with me;
    your rod and your staff, they comfort me.
[5]You prepare a table before me in the presence of my enemies;
    you anoint my head with oil, and my cup is running over.
[6]Surely goodness and mercy shall follow me
    all the days of my life,
    and I will dwell in the house of the LORD forever.

Psalm 27:1-3, 7, 9-14

[1]The LORD is my light and my salvation; whom then shall I fear?
    The LORD is the stronghold of my life;
    of whom shall I be afraid?
[2]When evildoers close in against me to devour my flesh,
    they, my foes and my enemies, will stumble and fall.
[3]Though an army encamp against me, my heart will not fear.
    Though war rise up against me,
    my trust will not be shaken.
[7]Hear my voice, O LORD, when I call;
    have mercy on me and answer me.
[9]Cast me not away—you have been my helper;
    forsake me not, O God of my salvation.
[10]Though my father and my mother forsake me,
    the LORD will take me in.
[11]Teach me your way, O LORD;
    lead me on a level path, because of my oppressors.

¹²Subject me not to the will of my foes,

> for they rise up against me, false witnesses
> breathing violence.

¹³This I believe—that I will see the goodness of the Lord

> in the land of the living!

¹⁴Wait for the Lord and be strong.

> Take heart and wait for the Lord!

Psalm 31:1-3, 9-17, 24

¹In you, O Lord, have I taken refuge; let me never be

> put to shame;
> deliver me in your righteousness.

²Incline your ear to me;

> make haste to deliver me.

³Be my strong rock, a castle to keep me safe,

> for you are my crag and my stronghold;
> for the sake of your name, lead me and guide me.

⁹Have mercy on me, O Lord, for I am in trouble;

> my eye is consumed with sorrow,
> and also my throat and my belly.

¹⁰For my life is wasted with grief, and my years with sighing;

> my strength fails me because of affliction, and my bones
> are consumed.

¹¹I am the scorn of all my enemies, a disgrace to my neighbors,

> a dismay to my acquaintances;
> when they see me in the street they avoid me.

¹²Like the dead I am forgotten, out of mind;

> I am as useless as a broken pot.

¹³For I have heard the whispering of the crowd;

> fear is all around;
> they put their heads together against me;
> they plot to take my life.

¹⁴But as for me, I have trusted in you, O Lord.

> I have said, "You are my God.

[15]My times are in your hand;

     rescue me from the hand of my enemies,

     and from those who persecute me.

[16]Let your face shine upon your servant;

     save me in your steadfast love."

[17]Lord, let me not be put to shame, for I have called on you;

     rather, let the wicked be put to shame; let them be

     silenced by the grave.

[24]Be strong and let your heart take courage,

     all you who wait for the Lord.

Psalm 34:1-8, 18, 22

[1]I will bless the Lord at all times;

     the praise of God shall ever be in my mouth.

[2]I will glory in the Lord;

     let the lowly hear and rejoice.

[3]Proclaim with me the greatness of the Lord;

     let us exalt God's name together.

[4]I sought the Lord, who answered me

     and delivered me from all my terrors.

[5]Look upon the Lord and be radiant,

     and let not your faces be ashamed.

[6]I called in my affliction, and the Lord heard me

     and saved me from all my troubles.

[7]The angel of the Lord encamps around those who

     fear the Lord

     and delivers them.

[8]Taste and see that the Lord is good;

     happy are they who take refuge in God!

[18]The Lord is near to the brokenhearted

     and saves those whose spirits are crushed.

[22]O Lord, you redeem the life of your servants,

     and those who put their trust in you will not be punished.

Psalm 42:1-5

[1]As the deer longs for the water-brooks,
    so longs my soul for you, O God.

[2]I thirst for God, for the living God;
    when shall I come to appear before the presence of God?

[3]My tears have been my food day and night,
    while all day long they say to me,
    "Where now is your God?"

[4]I pour out my soul when I think on these things;
    how I went with the multitude and led them into the
    house of God, with shouts of thanksgiving, among those
    keeping festival.

[5]Why are you so full of heaviness, O my soul, and why are you
    so disquieted within me?
    Put your trust in God, for I will yet give thanks to the one
    who is my help and my God.

Psalm 46

[1]God is our refuge and strength,
    a very present help in trouble.

[2]Therefore we will not fear, though the earth be moved,
    and though the mountains shake in the depths of the sea;

[3]though its waters rage and foam,
    and though the mountains tremble with its tumult.

[4]There is a river whose streams make glad the city of God,
    the holy habitation of the Most High.

[5]God is in the midst of the city; it shall not be shaken;
    God shall help it at the break of day.

[6]The nations rage, and the kingdoms shake;
    God speaks, and the earth melts away.

[7]The Lord of hosts is with us;
    the God of Jacob is our stronghold.

[8]Come now, regard the works of the LORD,
    what desolations God has brought upon the earth;
[9]behold the one who makes war to cease in all the world;
    who breaks the bow, and shatters the spear,
    and burns the shields with fire.
[10]"Be still, then, and know that I am God;
    I will be exalted among the nations;
    I will be exalted in the earth."
[11]The LORD of hosts is with us;
    the God of Jacob is our stronghold.

Psalm 51:1-12
[1]Have mercy on me, O God, according to your steadfast love;
    in your great compassion blot out my offenses.
[2]Wash me through and through from my wickedness,
    and cleanse me from my sin.
[3]For I know my offenses,
    and my sin is ever before me.
[4]Against you only have I sinned
    and done what is evil in your sight;
    so you are justified when you speak
    and right in your judgment.
[5]Indeed, I was born steeped in wickedness,
    a sinner from my mother's womb.
[6]Indeed, you delight in truth deep within me,
    and would have me know wisdom deep within.
[7]Remove my sins with hyssop, and I shall be clean;
    wash me, and I shall be purer than snow.
[8]Let me hear joy and gladness;
    that the body you have broken may rejoice.
[9]Hide your face from my sins,
    and blot out all my wickedness.

¹⁰Create in me a clean heart, O God,
 and renew a right spirit within me.
¹¹Cast me not away from your presence,
 and take not your Holy Spirit from me.
¹²Restore to me the joy of your salvation
 and sustain me with your bountiful Spirit.

Psalm 66:1-12; 20

¹Be joyful in God, all you lands;
 be joyful, all the earth.
²Sing the glory of God's name;
 sing the glory of God's praise.
³Say to God, "How awesome are your deeds!
 Because of your great strength
 your enemies cringe before you.
⁴All the earth bows down before you,
 sings to you, sings out your name."
⁵Come now and see the works of God,
 how awesome are God's deeds toward all people.
⁶God turned the sea into dry land,
 so that they went through the water on foot,
 and there we rejoiced in God.
⁷Ruling forever in might, God keeps watch over the nations;
 let no rebels exalt themselves.
⁸Bless our God, you peoples;
 let the sound of praise be heard.
⁹Our God has kept us among the living
 and has not allowed our feet to slip.
¹⁰For you, O God, have tested us;
 you have tried us just as silver is tried.
¹¹You brought us into the net;
 you laid heavy burdens upon our backs.

¹²You let people ride over our heads; we went through fire
and water,
but you brought us out into a place of refreshment.
²⁰Blessed be God, who has not rejected my prayer,
nor withheld unfailing love from me.

Psalm 71:1-12

¹In you, O LORD, have I taken refuge;
let me never be put to shame.
²In your righteousness, deliver me and set me free;
incline your ear to me and save me.
³Be my strong rock, a castle to keep me safe;
you are my crag and my stronghold.
⁴Deliver me, my God, from the hand of the wicked,
from the clutches of the evildoer and the oppressor.
⁵For you are my hope, O LORD God,
my confidence since I was young.
⁶I have been sustained by you ever since I was born; from my
mother's womb you have been my strength;
my praise shall be always of you.
⁷I have become a portent to many;
but you are my refuge and my strength.
⁸Let my mouth be full of your praise
and your glory all the day long.
⁹Do not cast me off in my old age;
forsake me not when my strength fails.
¹⁰For my enemies are talking against me,
and those who lie in wait for my life take
counsel together.
¹¹They say, "Pursue and seize that one whom God has forsaken;
because there is none who will save."
¹²O God, be not far from me;
come quickly to help me, O my God.

Psalm 88:1-13

[1]O Lord, my God, my Savior,
     by day and night I cry to you.
[2]Let my prayer enter into your presence;
     incline your ear to my lamentation.
[3]For I am full of trouble;
     my life is at the brink of the grave.
[4]I am counted among those who go down to the pit;
     I have become like one who has no strength;
[5]lost among the dead, like the slain who lie in the grave,
     whom you remember no more,
     for they are cut off from your hand.
[6]You have laid me in the depths of the pit,
     in dark places, and in the abyss.
[7]Your anger weighs upon me heavily,
     and all your great waves overwhelm me.
[8]You have put my friends far from me;
     you have made me to be abhorred by them;
     I am in prison and cannot get free.
[9]My sight has failed me because of trouble;
     Lord, I have called upon you daily;
     I have stretched out my hands to you.
[10]Do you work wonders for the dead?
     Will those who have died stand up and give you thanks?
[11]Will your lovingkindness be declared in the grave,
     your faithfulness in the land of destruction?
[12]Will your wonders be known in the dark
     or your righteousness in the country where all is
     forgotten?
[13]But as for me, O Lord, I cry to you for help;
     in the morning my prayer comes before you.

Psalm 91:1-7, 11-16

[1]You who dwell in the shelter of the Most High,
    who abide in the shadow of the Almighty—
[2]you will say to the Lord, "My refuge and my stronghold,
    my God in whom I put my trust."
[3]For God will rescue you from the snare of the hunter
    and from the deadly plague.
[4]God's wings will cover you,
    and you will find refuge beneath them;
    God's faithfulness will be your shield and defense.
[5]You shall not fear any terror in the night,
    nor the arrow that flies by day;
[6]nor the plague that stalks in the darkness,
    nor the sickness that lays waste at noon.
[7]A thousand may fall at your side
    and ten thousand at your right hand,
    but it will not come near you.
[11]For God will give the angels charge over you,
    to guard you in all your ways.
[12]Upon their hands they will bear you up,
    lest you strike your foot against a stone.
[13]You will tread upon the lion cub and viper;
    you will trample down the lion and the serpent.
[14]I will deliver those who cling to me;
    I will uphold them, because they know my name.
[15]They will call me, and I will answer them;
    I will be with them in trouble; I will rescue and
    honor them.
[16]With long life will I satisfy them,
    and show them my salvation.

Psalm 103:1-5, 8-18

[1]Bless the LORD, O my soul,
     and all that is within me, bless God's holy name.
[2]Bless the LORD, O my soul,
     and forget not all God's benefits—
[3]who forgives all your sins
     and heals all your diseases;
[4]who redeems your life from the grave
     and crowns you with steadfast love and mercy;
[5]who satisfies your desires with good things
     so that your youth is renewed like an eagle's.
[8]LORD, you are full of compassion and mercy,
     slow to anger and abounding in steadfast love;
[9]you will not always accuse us,
     nor will you keep your anger forever.
[10]You have not dealt with us according to our sins,
     nor repaid us according to our iniquities.
[11]For as the heavens are high above the earth,
     so great is your steadfast love for those who fear you.
[12]As far as the east is from the west,
     so far have you removed our transgressions from us.
[13]As a father has compassion for his children,
     so you have compassion for those who fear you, O LORD.
[14]For you know well how we are formed;
     you remember that we are but dust.
[15]As for mortals, their days are like the grass;
     they flourish like a flower of the field;
[16]when the wind passes over it, it is gone,
     and its place shall know it no more.
[17]But your steadfast love, O LORD,
     is forever with those who fear you,
     and your righteousness is for the children's children;
[18]for those who keep your covenant
     and remember to do your commandments.

Psalm 116:1-17

[1]I love the LORD, who has heard my voice,
    and listened to my supplication,
[2]for the LORD has given ear to me
    whenever I called.
[3]The cords of death entangled me;
    the anguish of the grave came upon me;
    I came to grief and sorrow.
[4]Then I called upon the name of the LORD:
    "O LORD, I pray you, save my life."
[5]Gracious is the LORD and righteous;
    our God is full of compassion.
[6]The LORD watches over the innocent;
    I was brought low, and God saved me.
[7]Turn again to your rest, O my soul.
    for the LORD has dealt well with you.
[8]For you have rescued my life from death,
    my eyes from tears, and my feet from stumbling;
[9]I will walk in the presence of the LORD
    in the land of the living.
[10]I believed, even when I said,
    "I am greatly afflicted."
[11]In my distress I said,
    "No one can be trusted."
[12]How shall I repay the LORD
    for all the good things God has done for me?
[13]I will lift the cup of salvation
    and call on the name of the LORD.
[14]I will fulfill my vows to the LORD
    in the presence of all God's people.
[15]Precious in your sight, O LORD,
    is the death of your servants.

[16]O LORD, truly I am your servant;

    I am your servant, the child of your handmaid;

    you have freed me from my bonds.

[17]I will offer you the sacrifice of thanksgiving

    and call upon the name of the LORD.

Psalm 121 (See page 137)

Psalm 130

[1]Out of the depths

    I cry to you, O LORD;

[2]O LORD, hear my voice!

    Let your ears be attentive to the voice of my supplication.

[3]If you were to keep watch over sins,

    O LORD, who could stand?

[4]Yet with you is forgiveness,

    in order that you may be feared.

[5]I wait for you, O LORD; my soul waits;

    in your word is my hope.

[6]My soul waits for the LORD

    more than those who keep watch for the morning,

    more than those who keep watch for the morning.

[7]O Israel, wait for the LORD,

    for with the LORD there is steadfast love;

    with the LORD there is plenteous redemption.

[8]For the LORD shall redeem Israel

    from all their sins.

Psalm 139:1-17, 23-24

[1]LORD, you have searched me out;

    O LORD, you have known me.

[2]You know my sitting down and my rising up;

    you discern my thoughts from afar.

³You trace my journeys and my resting-places
    and are acquainted with all my ways.
⁴Indeed, there is not a word on my lips,
    but you, O Lᴏʀᴅ, know it altogether.
⁵You encompass me, behind and before,
    and lay your hand upon me.
⁶Such knowledge is too wonderful for me;
    it is so high that I cannot attain to it.
⁷Where can I go then from your Spirit?
    Where can I flee from your presence?
⁸If I climb up to heaven, you are there;
    if I make the grave my bed, you are there also.
⁹If I take the wings of the morning
    and dwell in the uttermost parts of the sea,
¹⁰even there your hand will lead me
    and your right hand hold me fast.
¹¹If I say, "Surely the darkness will cover me,
    and the light around me turn to night,"
¹²darkness is not dark to you; the night is as bright as the day;
    darkness and light to you are both alike.
¹³For you yourself created my inmost parts;
    you knit me together in my mother's womb.
¹⁴I will thank you because I am marvelously made;
    your works are wonderful, and I know it well.
¹⁵My body was not hidden from you,
    while I was being made in secret
    and woven in the depths of the earth.
¹⁶Your eyes beheld my limbs, yet unfinished in the womb;
    all of them were written in your book;
    my days were fashioned before they came to be.
¹⁷How deep I find your thoughts, O God!
    How great is the sum of them!

[23]Search me out, O God, and know my heart;
　　try me and know my restless thoughts.
[24]Look well whether there be any wickedness in me
　　and lead me in the way that is everlasting.

Psalm 146

[1]Hallelujah!
　　Praise the LORD, O my soul!
[2]I will praise the LORD as long as I live;
　　I will sing praises to my God while I have my being.
[3]Put not your trust in rulers,
　　in mortals in whom there is no help.
[4]When they breathe their last, they return to earth,
　　and in that day their thoughts perish.
[5]Happy are they who have the God of Jacob for their help,
　　whose hope is in the LORD their God;
[6]who made heaven and earth, the seas, and all that is in them;
　　who keeps promises forever;
[7]who gives justice to those who are oppressed,
　　and food to those who hunger.
　　The LORD sets the captive free.
[8]The LORD opens the eyes of the blind;
　　the LORD lifts up those who are bowed down;
　　the LORD loves the righteous.
[9]The LORD cares for the stranger;
　　the LORD sustains the orphan and widow,
　　but frustrates the way of the wicked.
[10]The LORD shall reign forever,
　　your God, O Zion, throughout all generations. Hallelujah!

God Is My Advocate

Peace I leave with you;
my peace I give to you. I do not
give to you as the world gives. Do
not let your hearts be troubled,
and do not let them be afraid.

—John 14:27

TOPICAL SCRIPTURE SUGGESTIONS

Addiction/Recovery
See related prayer on page 116.
Psalm 40:1-3 *I waited patiently on the Lord*
2 Corinthians 4:6-10 *Treasure in clay jars*

Anger
See related prayer on page 110.
Ephesians 4:26 *Do not let the sun go down on your anger*
James 1:19-20 *Be slow to anger*

Christian Life
See related prayers on page 118.
Matthew 6:25-27, 33-34 *Do not be anxious*
Romans 12:14-21 *Live in harmony with one another*
Galatians 5:22-23 *The fruits of the Spirit*
Colossians 3:12-15 *Above all, clothe yourselves with love*

Courage/Perseverance
See related prayer on page 114.
Psalm 31:1-5 (see page 194)
John 16:33 *Take courage*
Romans 8:28 *All things work together for good*
1 Corinthians 10:12-13 *God is faithful*

Deliverance
Psalm 27 (page 193); Psalm 130 (page 204)
Zephaniah 3:16-19 *The Lord, your God, is in your midst*
2 Timothy 1:8-9, 12 *Relying on the power of God*

Despair
See related prayer/s on page 110, 112.
Psalm 88 (page 200); Psalm 130 (page 204)
Matthew 11:28-30 *I will give you rest*
1 Peter 5:7-10 *Cast your anxieties on God*

Encouragement
Ephesians 6:10-18 *Strength in the Lord*
Hebrews 12:1-3 *Surrounded by a cloud of witnesses*

Everlasting Life
John 14:1-3 *I prepare a place for you*

Faith
Psalm 23 (page 193); Psalm 27 (page 193)
Mark 9:24 *Help my unbelief*
Hebrews 11:1 *Assurance of things hoped for*

Fear/Courage
See related prayer on page 111.
Deuteronomy 31:6 *Be strong*
Isaiah 41:10 *Do not be afraid*

God's Nature
Psalm 86:15 *God is merciful and gracious*
Isaiah 55:8-9 *My thoughts are not your thoughts*
Lamentations 3:22-25 *The steadfast love of the Lord*
Hebrews 12:28-29 *God is a consuming fire*

Guidance
See related prayer on page 114.
Genesis 28:15-16 *Know that I am with you*
Isaiah 30:19-21 *This is the way*
Matthew 11:28-30 *I will give you rest*

Guilt and Forgiveness
See related prayer/s on page 113, 114.
Psalm 51 (page 197)
Isaiah 55:6-7 *Seek the Lord*
Romans 3:22-24 *All have sinned and fallen short*
1 John 1:8-9 *If we confess our sin, God is faithful and just*

Holy Spirit
John 14:16-18 *Spirit of truth*
Romans 8:26 *The Spirit intercedes for us*

Hope
Jeremiah 29:11 *Surely I know the plans I have for you*
Romans 8:24-25 *In hope we were saved*

Illness
See related prayer on page 112.
Psalm 23 (page 193); Psalm 91 (page 201)
Mark 5:24-34 *Be healed*
James 5:13-16 *Pray for one another, so that you may be healed*

Imprisonment
Psalm 146 (page 206)
Matthew 25:31-40 *I was in prison and you visited me*
Luke 4:16-21 *Proclaim release to the captives*
Luke 21:12-19 *Not a hair on your head will perish*
Acts 12:1-10 *Peter in prison*
Philippians 1:12-20 *Paul in prison*
2 Timothy 2:8-9 *The word of God is not chained*
Hebrews 11:1-3, 30-36 *Assurance of things hoped for*
Hebrews 13:1, 3 *Remember those who are in prison*

Jesus
See also "Praying through the Year" (pages 13–102)
John 1:1-5 *In the beginning was the Word*
John 3:16 *God so loved the world*
Philippians 2:5-11 *Jesus humbled himself*

Justice
Micah 6:8 *Do justice, love kindness, walk humbly*
Luke 18:1-8 *God grants justice*

Loneliness
See related prayer on page 109.
Psalm 23 (page 193); Psalm 42 (page 196)
Isaiah 49:13b-16 *God will not forget you*

Love
John 15:7-11 *Abide in my love*
1 Corinthians 13:1-8, 13 *The greatest of these is love*
1 John 4:7-12 *Love is from God*

Mental Illness
See related prayer on page 111.
Psalm 88 (page 200); Psalm 130 (page 204)
Romans 8:18, 22-27 *Creation will be set free*

Peace
Numbers 6:24-26 *The Lord gives you peace*
John 14:25-27 *Peace I leave with you*

Praise and Thanksgiving
See related prayer on page 115.
Psalm 66 (page 198); Psalm 103 (page 202)
Philippians 4:4-7 *The peace of God will guard your hearts*

Prayer
Jeremiah 29:12-14 *Seek me with all your heart*
Matthew 7:7-11 *Ask, and it will be given you*
Luke 11:1-4 *Lord, teach us to pray*
Ephesians 6:18-20 *Pray in the Spirit*
Philippians 4:6-7 *Let your requests be made known*

Rescue
Mark 4:35-41 *Jesus stills the storm*

Separation from Loved Ones
See also "Praying Inside with Those Outside" (pages 126–130)
Genesis 31:44-46, 48-49 *The Lord watch between you and me*
Mark 10:13-16 *Let the children come*

Shame
See related prayer on page 106.
John 8:3-11 *I do not condemn you*

Suffering
Romans 5:1-5 *Justification by faith gives peace with God*
Romans 8:14-18 *We are children of God*
1 Corinthians 10:13 *God is faithful*

Temptation
See also Lent 2: Guidance through the Journey (page 58)
Luke 4:1-12 *The temptation of Jesus*

Trust
Psalm 139 (page 204); Psalm 146:5-7 (page 206)
Deuteronomy 31:6 *The LORD your God goes with you*
Habakkuk 3:17-19 *God, the LORD, is my strength*
John 14:1 *Do not let your hearts be troubled*

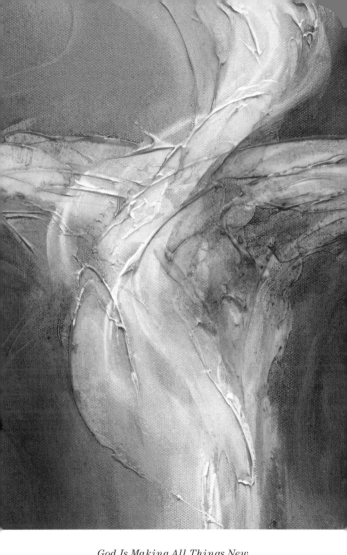

God Is Making All Things New

Do not remember the former things or consider the things of old. I am about to do a new thing; now it springs forth, do you perceive it?

—*Isaiah 43:18-19*

HYMNS AND SONGS

1 Hark! The Herald Angels Sing

1   Hark! The herald angels sing,
    "Glory to the newborn king;
    peace on earth, and mercy mild,
    God and sinners reconciled."
    Joyful, all you nations, rise;
    join the triumph of the skies;
    with angelic hosts proclaim,
    "Christ is born in Bethlehem!"

    Refrain
    Hark! The herald angels sing,
    "Glory to the newborn king!"

2   Hail the heav'n-born Prince of peace!
    Hail the Sun of righteousness!
    Light and life to all he brings,
    ris'n with healing in his wings.
    Mild he lays his glory by,
    born that we no more may die,
    born to raise each child of earth,
    born to give us second birth. *Refrain*

Charles Wesley, 1707-1788, alt.

2 Silent Night, Holy Night!

1 Silent night, holy night!
   All is calm, all is bright
   round yon virgin mother and child.
   Holy Infant, so tender and mild,
   sleep in heavenly peace,
   sleep in heavenly peace.

2 Silent night, holy night!
   Shepherds quake at the sight;
   glories stream from heaven afar,
   heav'nly hosts sing, alleluia!
   Christ, the Savior, is born!
   Christ, the Savior, is born!

3 Silent night, holy night!
   Son of God, love's pure light
   radiant beams from your holy face,
   with the dawn of redeeming grace,
   Jesus, Lord, at your birth,
   Jesus, Lord, at your birth.

Joseph Mohr, 1792-1849; tr. John F. Young, 1820-1885

3 O Come, All Ye Faithful

1 O come, all ye faithful,
   joyful and triumphant!
   O come ye, O come ye to Bethlehem;
   come and behold him,
   born the king of angels:

   Refrain
   O come, let us adore him,
   O come, let us adore him,
   O come, let us adore him, Christ the Lord!

2 Yea, Lord, we greet thee,
   born this happy morning;
   Jesus, to thee be glory giv'n!
   Word of the Father,
   now in flesh appearing: *Refrain*

attr. John Francis Wade, 1711-1786; tr. composite

4 O Sacred Head, Now Wounded

1 O sacred head, now wounded,
with grief and shame weighed down,
now scornfully surrounded
with thorns, thine only crown;
O sacred head, what glory,
what bliss till now was thine!
Yet, though despised and gory,
I joy to call thee mine.

2 What language shall I borrow
to thank thee, dearest friend,
for this thy dying sorrow,
thy pity without end?
Oh, make me thine forever,
and should I fainting be,
Lord, let me never, never
outlive my love to thee.

3 Lord, be my consolation;
shield me when I must die;
remind me of thy passion
when my last hour draws nigh.
These eyes, new faith receiving,
from thee shall never move;
for all who die believing
die safely in thy love.

Paul Gerhardt, 1607-1676, based on Arnulf of Louvain, d. 1250; tr. composite

5 Jesus Christ Is Risen Today

1 Jesus Christ is ris'n today, Alleluia!
   our triumphant holy day, Alleluia!
   who did once upon the cross, Alleluia!
   suffer to redeem our loss. Alleluia!

2 But the pains which he endured, Alleluia!
   our salvation have procured; Alleluia!
   now above the sky he's king, Alleluia!
   where the angels ever sing. Alleluia!

3 Sing we to our God above, Alleluia!
   praise eternal as his love; Alleluia!
   praise him, all you heav'nly host, Alleluia!
   Father, Son, and Holy Ghost. Alleluia!

Latin, 14th cent., sts. 1-3; tr. J. Walsh, Lyra Davidica, 1708, alt.;
Charles Wesley, 1707-1788, st. 4

6 Come by Here

1 Come by here, my Lord, come by here;
   come by here, my Lord, come by here;
   come by here, my Lord, come by here;
   O Lord, come by here.

2 Someone's crying, Lord, come by here ...
3 Someone's singing, Lord, come by here ...
4 Someone's praying, Lord, come by here ...
5 Someone needs you, Lord, come by here ...

Traditional

7 Let Us Break Bread Together

1 Let us break bread together on our knees;
let us break bread together on our knees.

Refrain
When I fall on my knees,
with my face to the rising sun,
O Lord, have mercy on me.

2 Let us drink wine together on our knees ...

3 Let us praise God together on our knees ...

African American spiritual

8 A Mighty Fortress Is Our God

1 A mighty fortress is our God,
a sword and shield victorious;
he breaks the cruel oppressor's rod
and wins salvation glorious.
The old satanic foe
has sworn to work us woe!
With craft and dreadful might
he arms himself to fight.
On earth he has no equal.

2 No strength of ours can match his might!
We would be lost, rejected.
But now a champion comes to fight,
whom God himself elected.
You ask who this may be?
The Lord of hosts is he!
Christ Jesus, mighty Lord,
God's only Son, adored.
He holds the field victorious.

Martin Luther, 1483-1546; tr. Lutheran Book of Worship

9 There's a Wideness in God's Mercy

1 There's a wideness in God's mercy,
   like the wideness of the sea;
   there's a kindness in God's justice
   which is more than liberty.
   There is no place where earth's sorrows
   are more felt than up in heav'n.
   There is no place where earth's failings
   have such kindly judgment giv'n.

2 There is welcome for the sinner,
   and a promised grace made good;
   there is mercy with the Savior;
   there is healing in his blood.
   There is grace enough for thousands
   of new worlds as great as this;
   there is room for fresh creations
   in that upper home of bliss.

3 For the love of God is broader
   than the measures of our mind;
   and the heart of the Eternal
   is most wonderfully kind.
   But we make this love too narrow
   by false limits of our own;
   and we magnify its strictness
   with a zeal God will not own.

4 'Tis not all we owe to Jesus;
   it is something more than all:
   greater good because of evil,
   larger mercy through the fall.
   Make our love, O God, more faithful;
   let us take you at your word,
   and our lives will be thanksgiving
   for the goodness of the Lord.

Frederick W. Faber, 1814-1863, alt.

10 Just as I Am, without One Plea

1 Just as I am, without one plea,
  but that thy blood was shed for me,
  and that thou bidd'st me come to thee,
  O Lamb of God, I come, I come.

2 Just as I am, though tossed about
  with many a conflict, many a doubt,
  fightings and fears within, without,
  O Lamb of God, I come, I come.

3 Just as I am, thou wilt receive,
  wilt welcome, pardon, cleanse, relieve;
  because thy promise I believe,
  O Lamb of God, I come, I come.

4 Just as I am; thy love unknown
  has broken ev'ry barrier down;
  now to be thine, yea, thine alone,
  O Lamb of God, I come, I come.

Charlotte Elliott, 1789-1871

11 My Hope Is Built on Nothing Less

1 My hope is built on nothing less
  than Jesus' blood and righteousness;
  no merit of my own I claim,
  but wholly lean on Jesus' name.

  Refrain
  On Christ, the solid rock, I stand;
  all other ground is sinking sand.

2 His oath, his covenant, his blood
  sustain me in the raging flood;
  when all supports are washed away,
  he then is all my hope and stay. *Refrain*

3 When he shall come with trumpet sound,
  oh, may I then in him be found,
  clothed in his righteousness alone,
  redeemed to stand before the throne! *Refrain*

Edward Mote, 1797-1874, alt.

12 Abide with Me

1 Abide with me, fast falls the eventide.
The darkness deepens; Lord, with me abide.
When other helpers fail and comforts flee,
help of the helpless, oh, abide with me.

2 I need thy presence ev'ry passing hour;
what but thy grace can foil the tempter's pow'r?
Who like thyself my guide and stay can be?
Through cloud and sunshine, oh, abide with me.

3 I fear no foe, with thee at hand to bless;
ills have no weight, and tears no bitterness.
Where is death's sting? Where, grave, thy victory?
I triumph still, if thou abide with me!

4 Hold thou thy cross before my closing eyes,
shine through the gloom, and point me to the skies;
heav'n's morning breaks,
and earth's vain shadows flee;
in life, in death, O Lord, abide with me.

Henry F. Lyte, 1793-1847

13 O God, Our Help in Ages Past

1 O God, our help in ages past,
   our hope for years to come,
   our shelter from the stormy blast,
   and our eternal home:

2 Under the shadow of your throne
   your saints have dwelt secure;
   sufficient is your arm alone,
   and our defense is sure.

3 Before the hills in order stood
   or earth received its frame,
   from everlasting you are God,
   to endless years the same.

4 A thousand ages in your sight
   are like an evening gone,
   short as the watch that ends the night
   before the rising sun.

5 Time, like an ever-rolling stream,
   bears all our years away;
   they fly forgotten, as a dream
   dies at the op'ning day.

6 O God, our help in ages past,
   our hope for years to come,
   still be our guard while troubles last
   and our eternal home.

Isaac Watts, 1674-1748, alt.

14 Blessed Assurance

1 Blessed assurance, Jesus is mine!
   Oh, what a foretaste of glory divine!
   Heir of salvation, purchase of God,
   born of his Spirit, washed in his blood.

   Refrain
   This is my story, this is my song,
   praising my Savior, all the day long:
   this is my story, this is my song,
   praising my Savior all the day long.

2 Perfect submission, perfect delight,
   visions of rapture now burst on my sight;
   angels descending bring from above
   echoes of mercy, whispers of love. *Refrain*

3 Perfect submission, all is at rest;
   I in my Savior am happy and blest,
   watching and waiting, looking above,
   filled with his goodness, lost in his love. *Refrain*

Fanny J. Crosby, 1820-1915

15 How Long, O God

1 "How long, O God?" the psalmist cries,
   a cry we make our own,
   for we are lost, alone, afraid,
   and far away from home.

2 The evil lurks within, without,
   it threatens to destroy
   the fragile cords that make us one,
   that bind our hearts in joy.

3 Your grace, O God, seems far away;
   will healing ever come?
   Our broken lives lie broken still;
   will night give way to dawn?

4 How can we hope? How can we sing?
   O God, set free our voice
   to name the sorrows, name the pain,
   that we might yet rejoice.

5 "How long, O God?" the psalmist cries,
     a cry we make our own.
     Though we are lost, alone, afraid,
     our God will lead us home.

Ralph F. Smith, 1950-1994 © 2003 Augsburg Fortress

16 Mothering God, You Gave Me Birth

1 Mothering God, you gave me birth
     in the bright morning of this world.
     Creator, source of ev'ry breath,
     you are my rain, my wind, my sun.

2 Mothering Christ, you took my form,
     offering me your food of light,
     grain of life, and grape of love,
     your very body for my peace.

3 Mothering Spirit, nurt'ring one,
     in arms of patience hold me close,
     so that in faith I root and grow
     until I flow'r, until I know.

Jean Janzen, b. 1933; based on Julian of Norwich, c. 1342-c. 1413
Text © 1991 Jean Janzen, admin. Augsburg Fortress

17 What a Friend We Have in Jesus

1 What a friend we have in Jesus,
all our sins and griefs to bear!
What a privilege to carry
ev'rything to God in prayer!
Oh, what peace we often forfeit;
oh, what needless pain we bear—
all because we do not carry
ev'rything to God in prayer!

2 Have we trials and temptations?
Is there trouble anywhere?
We should never be discouraged—
take it to the Lord in prayer.
Can we find a friend so faithful
who will all our sorrows share?
Jesus knows our ev'ry weakness—
take it to the Lord in prayer.

3 Are we weak and heavy-laden,
cumbered with a load of care?
Precious Savior, still our refuge—
take it to the Lord in prayer.
Do your friends despise, forsake you?
Take it to the Lord in prayer.
In his arms he'll take and shield you;
you will find a solace there.

Joseph Scriven, 1820-1886

18 It's Me, O Lord
Standing in the Need of Prayer

Refrain
It's me, it's me, O Lord,
standin' in the need of prayer;
it's me, it's me, O Lord,
standin' in the need of prayer.

1 Not my brother, not my sister,
but it's me, O Lord,
standin' in the need of prayer ... *Refrain*

2 Not the preacher, not the deacon,
   but it's me, O Lord,
   standin' in the need of prayer ... *Refrain*

3 Not my father, not my mother,
   but it's me, O Lord,
   standin' in the need of prayer ... *Refrain*

4 Not the stranger, not my neighbor,
   but it's me, O Lord,
   standin' in the need of prayer ... *Refrain*

   African American spiritual

19 Amazing Grace, How Sweet the Sound

1 Amazing grace! how sweet the sound
   that saved a wretch like me!
   I once was lost, but now am found;
   was blind, but now I see.

2 'Twas grace that taught my heart to fear,
   and grace my fears relieved;
   how precious did that grace appear
   the hour I first believed!

3 Through many dangers, toils, and snares
   I have already come;
   'tis grace has brought me safe thus far,
   and grace will lead me home.

4 The Lord has promised good to me;
   his word my hope secures;
   he will my shield and portion be
   as long as life endures.

5 When we've been there ten thousand years,
   bright shining as the sun,
   we've no less days to sing God's praise
   than when we'd first begun.

   John Newton, 1725-1807, alt., sts. 1-4; anonymous, st. 5

20 Now Thank We All Our God

1 Now thank we all our God
   with hearts and hands and voices,
   who wondrous things has done,
   in whom this world rejoices;
   who, from our mothers' arms,
   has blest us on our way
   with countless gifts of love,
   and still is ours today.

2 Oh, may this bounteous God
   through all our life be near us,
   with ever joyful hearts
   and blessed peace to cheer us,
   and keep us all in grace,
   and guide us when perplexed,
   and free us from all harm
   in this world and the next.

3 All praise and thanks to God
   the Father now be given,
   the Son, and Spirit blest,
   who reign in highest heaven,
   the one eternal God,
   whom earth and heav'n adore;
   for thus it was, is now,
   and shall be evermore.

Martin Rinkhart, 1586-1649; tr. Catherine Winkworth, 1827-1878

21 Lift Every Voice and Sing

1 Lift ev'ry voice and sing till earth and heaven ring,
 ring with the harmonies of liberty.
 Let our rejoicing rise high as the list'ning skies,
 let it resound loud as the rolling sea.
 Sing a song full of the faith that the dark past has taught us;
 sing a song full of the hope that the present has brought us;
 facing the rising sun of our new day begun,
 let us march on till victory is won.

2 Stony the road we trod, bitter the chast'ning rod,
 felt in the days when hope unborn had died;
 yet with a steady beat, have not our weary feet
 come to the place for which our parents sighed?
 We have come over a way that with tears has been watered;
 we have come, treading our path through the blood
  of the slaughtered,
 out from the gloomy past, till now we stand at last
 where the white gleam of our bright star is cast.

3 God of our weary years, God of our silent tears,
 thou who hast brought us thus far on the way;
 thou who hast by thy might led us into the light,
 keep us forever in the path, we pray.
 Lest our feet stray from the places, our God, where we met thee;
 lest, our hearts drunk with the wine of the world, we forget thee;
 shadowed beneath thy hand may we forever stand,
 true to our God, true to our native land.

James W. Johnson, 1871-1938

DATES FOR THE CHURCH YEAR 2019–2050

	FIRST SUNDAY IN ADVENT	ASH WEDNESDAY	GOOD FRIDAY	EASTER	PENTECOST
2019	12/1	3/6	4/19	4/21	6/9
2020	11/29	2/26	4/10	4/12	5/31
2021	11/28	2/17	4/2	4/4	5/23
2022	11/27	3/2	4/15	4/17	6/5
2023	12/3	2/22	4/7	4/9	5/28
2024	12/1	2/14	3/29	3/31	5/19
2025	11/30	3/5	4/18	4/20	6/8
2026	11/29	2/18	4/3	4/5	5/24
2027	11/28	2/10	3/26	3/28	5/16
2028	12/3	3/1	4/14	4/16	6/4
2029	12/2	2/14	3/30	4/1	5/20
2030	12/1	3/6	4/19	4/21	6/9
2031	11/30	2/26	4/11	4/13	6/1
2032	11/28	2/11	3/26	3/28	5/16
2033	11/27	3/2	4/15	4/17	6/5
2034	12/3	2/22	4/7	4/9	5/28
2035	12/2	2/7	3/23	3/25	5/13
2036	11/30	2/27	4/11	4/13	6/1
2037	11/29	2/18	4/3	4/5	5/24
2038	11/28	3/10	4/23	4/25	6/13
2039	11/27	2/23	4/8	4/10	5/29
2040	12/2	2/15	3/30	4/1	5/20
2041	12/1	3/6	4/19	4/21	6/9
2042	11/30	2/19	4/4	4/6	5/25
2043	11/29	2/11	3/27	3/29	5/17
2044	11/27	3/2	4/15	4/17	6/5
2045	12/3	2/22	4/7	4/9	5/28
2046	12/2	2/7	3/23	3/25	5/13
2047	12/1	2/27	4/12	4/14	5/2
2048	11/29	2/19	4/3	4/5	5/24
2049	11/28	3/3	4/16	4/18	6/6
2050	11/27	2/23	4/8	4/10	5/29

ACKNOWLEDGMENTS

Editorial Team
Mitzi J. Budde and Jennifer Baker-Trinity, editors; Kevin L. Strickland, Martin A. Seltz

Contributors
Beth Bingham, Mitzi J. Budde, Bruce Burnside, Lenny Duncan, Linda Manson, Paul Palumbo, Gail Ramshaw, Peter Carlson Schattauer, Amanda Weber

Consultation and Review
Larry Evans, Julian Gordy, Josh Gribbon, Deb Haynes, Heidi Kugler, Luis Menéndez-Antuña, Mary Mortenson, Fred Nelson, Eric Wester

Design and Production
Robyn Sand Anderson, visual art; Tory Herman, Laurie Ingram, design

Evangelical Lutheran Church in America, *The Church and Criminal Justice: Hearing the Cries—A Social Statement on Criminal Justice*. The implementing resolutions of this social statement called for the development of this prayer book. The statement and other supplemental materials can be downloaded at elca.org/socialstatements.

SOURCES AND NOTES

Scripture quotations, except for quotations from the Psalms and as otherwise noted, are from the New Revised Standard Version Bible. © 1989 Division of Christian Education of the National Council of Churches of Christ in the United States of America. All rights reserved. Used by permission.

Quotations from the Psalms were prepared for *Evangelical Lutheran Worship* © 2006 Evangelical Lutheran Church in America, admin. Augsburg Fortress.

This resource incorporates materials from several Evangelical Lutheran Worship resources, abbreviated in this section as follows. Additional notes regarding these materials may be found in these volumes.

Evangelical Lutheran Worship, Augsburg Fortress, 2006 (ELW)
Evangelical Lutheran Worship Pastoral Care, Augsburg Fortress, 2009 (ELW-PC)
Evangelical Lutheran Worship Occasional Services, Augsburg Fortress, 2010 (ELW-OS)
Evangelical Lutheran Worship Prayer Book for the Armed Services, Augsburg Fortress, 2013 (ELW-PBAS)

[1] Thomas Merton, *Contemplative Prayer* (New York: Image, 1971), 37.
[2] Pierre Teilhard de Chardin, *The Making of a Mind: Letters from a Soldier-Priest 1914-1919* (New York: Harper & Row, 1961), 57.
[3] Rory Cooney, "Canticle of the Turning," in ELW, #723. Text ©1990 GIA Publications, Inc. Used by permission.
[4] Vincent van Gogh, Letter #638: "To Theo van Gogh. Arles, Monday, 9 or Tuesday, 10 July 1888," in *Vincent van Gogh: The Letters*: www.vangoghletters.org/vg/letters/let638/letter.html#translation.
[5] Langston Hughes, *The Collected Poems of Langston Hughes* (New York: Vintage Books, 1994), 32. Used by permission.
[6] Denise Levertov, "Annunciation," in *The Collected Poems of Denise Levertov* (New York: New Directions, 2013), 836.
[7] ELW, #251. Text © 1995 Augsburg Fortress.
[8] Dietrich Bonhoeffer, *Letters and Papers from Prison*, enlarged ed. (New York: Macmillan, 1972), 416.
[9] Eberhard Arnold, "When the Time Was Fulfilled," in *Watch for the Light: Readings for Advent and Christmas* (Maryknoll, NY: Plough Publishing House, 2001), 28.
[10] Frederick Buechner, *Secrets in the Dark: A Life in Sermons* (New York: Harper Collins Publishers, 2007), 24.
[11] Nadia Bolz-Weber, *Pastrix: The Cranky, Beautiful Faith of a Sinner & Saint* (New York: Jericho Books, 2013), 49.

[12] Marianne Williamson, *A Return to Love: Reflections on the Principles of "A Course in Miracles"* (New York: HarperCollins, 1993), 191.

[13] Nelson Mandela, *Long Walk to Freedom* (Boston: Little, Brown, 1994), 544.

[14] Desmond Tutu, *God Has a Dream: A Vision of Hope for Our Time* (New York: Doubleday, 2004), vii-viii.

[15] From a favorite song of the Voices of Hope choir, used with the author's permission.

[16] Jan Richardson, "Rend Your Heart," excerpt from *Circle of Grace: A Book of Blessings for the Seasons* (Orlando: Wanton Gospeller Press, 2015), 94. © Jan Richardson, janrichardson.com. Used by permission.

[17] Fred Rogers, *Life's Journeys according to Mister Rogers: Things to Remember along the Way* (New York: Hachette, 2014), 98.

[18] Bryan Stevenson, *Just Mercy* (New York: Speigel and Grau, 2014), 290.

[19] Fred Rogers, *Life's Journeys*, 36.

[20] Jan Richardson, "Palm Sunday: Blessing of Palms," in The Painted Prayerbook: paintedprayerbook.com/2017/04/05/palm-sunday-blessing-of-palms/.

[21] South African traditional, "We Are Marching in the Light/*Siyahamba*," in ELW, #866. Text tr. *Freedom Is Coming* © 1984 Utryck, admin. GIA Publications, Inc. Used by permission.

[22] Jonathan Swift, "Thoughts on Various Subjects," in *The Prose Works of Jonathan Swift, D.D.* (London: George Bell and Sons, 1907), v. 1, 272.

[23] Brian Wren, "Great God, Your Love Has Called Us," in ELW, #358. Text ©1977, rev.1995, Hope Publishing Company. Used by permission.

[24] William Sloane Coffin, *The Collected Sermons of William Sloane Coffin: The Riverside Years*, v. 2 (Louisville: Westminster John Knox, 2008), 4-5.

[25] Taizé Community "Stay with Me," in ELW, #348. Text ©1984 Les Presses de Taizé, admin. GIA Publications, Inc. Used by permission.

[26] Rowan Williams, *Tokens of Trust: An Introduction to Christian Belief* (Louisville, KY: Westminster John Knox, 2007), 91.

[27] Carrie Newcomer and Michael Maines, "Leaves Don't Drop," *Geography of Light* (Album), February 12, 2008. Used by permission.

[28] Maceo Woods, "We Won't Leave Here Like We Came," in *African American Heritage Hymnal* (Chicago: GIA Publications, Inc., 2001), #407. Text © Maceo Woods, admin. GIA Publications, Inc. Used by permission.

[29] Clarence Jordan, *Clarence Jordan Essential Writings* (Maryknoll: Orbis Books, 2003), 139-140.

[30] Alice Walker, *The Way Forward Is with a Broken Heart* (New York: Ballantine Books, 2000), 200.

[31] Michael Perry, "Heal Me, Hands of Jesus," in *The United Methodist Hymnal* (Nashville: The United Methodist Publishing House, 1989), #262. Text © 1982 Hope Publishing. Used by permission.

[32] Shauna Niequist, *Savor: Living Abundantly Where You Are, As You Are* (Grand Rapids, MI: Zondervan, 2015), 8.

33 James E. Moore Jr., "Taste and See," in ELW, #493. Text ©1983 GIA Publications, Inc. Used by permission.

34 Martin Luther King Jr., "Letter from Birmingham City Jail," in *A Testament of Hope: The Essential Writings of Martin Luther King Jr.*, ed. James Melvin Washington (San Francisco: Harper & Row, 1986), 300.

35 Michael Curry, "Sermon from the Royal Wedding," New York Times (May 19, 2018).

36 C. S. Lewis, *The Weight of Glory and Other Addresses* (New York: Simon and Schuster, 1996), 135.

37 Frederick Douglass, "The Life and Times of Frederick Douglass," in *Autobiographies* (New York: The Library of America, 1994), 540.

38 Nelson Mandela, *Long Walk to Freedom*, 341-42.

39 ELW-PBAS, 45.

40 Ibid.

41 ELW-PBAS, 46.

42 ELW, 304, adapt.

43 ELW-PBAS, 73.

44 ELW, 87.

45 Ibid.

46 ELW-OS, 398.

47 George Appleton, ed., *The Oxford Book of Prayer* (Oxford: Oxford University Press, 1985), 112.

48 ELW-OS, 399.

49 ELW, 305, alt.

50 ELW, 317.

51 ELW, 318, alt.

52 ELW, 326.

53 ELW, 326, alt.

54 *A New Zealand Prayer Book/He Karakia Mihinare o Aotearoa* (Auckland: William Collins, 1989), 184.

55 Anne Lamott, *Help, Thanks, Wow: The Three Essential Prayers* (New York: Riverhead, 2012).

56 Brother Lawrence of the Resurrection, *Writings and Conversations on the Practice of the Presence of God*, critical edition by Conrad De Meester, OCD (Washington, DC: ICS Publications, 1994), 63.

57 Thomas Kelly, *A Testament of Devotion* (New York: Harper & Brothers, 1941), 39.

58 The Episcopal Church, *Book of Common Prayer* (New York: Church Publishing., 1979), 461.

59 Inspired by "Litany of Remembrance and Lament, Healing and Hope" in The Episcopal Church, *Enriching Our Worship 5: Liturgies and Prayers Related to Childbearing, Childbirth, and Loss* (New York: Church Publishing, 2009), 42-47.

[60] Influenced by Yolanda Pierce, *A Litany for Those Who Aren't Ready for Healing*. www.yolandapierce.blogspot.com/2014/11/a-litany-for-those-whoarent-ready-for.html and using language suggested in Evangelical Lutheran Church in America, "A Social Statement on The Church and Criminal Justice: Hearing the Cries" (2013).

[61] ELW-PBAS, 144-150, adapt.

[62] Martin Luther, "Prefaces to the Old Testament," in *Luther's Works*, vol. 35 (Philadelphia: Muhlenberg, 1960), 236.

[63] Order of Carmelites, "What Is Lectio Divina?" www.ocarm.org/en/carmelites/what-lectio-divina.

[64] Adapted from the New Revised Standard Version.

[65] George H. Tavard, *The Spiritual Way of St. Jeanne d'Arc* (Collegeville, MN: Liturgical Press, 1998), 90.

[66] Cited in David Daniell, *William Tyndale: A Biography* (New Haven: Yale University Press, 1994), 379.

[67] Thomas Hutchinson, *The History of Massachusetts: From the First Settlement thereof in 1628, until the year 1750*, 3rd edition, v. 2, (Boston: Thomas and Andrews, 1795), 439-440.

[68] Dietrich Bonhoeffer, *Discipleship*. Dietrich Bonhoeffer Works, v. 4 (Minneapolis: Fortress, 2003), 87, 88.

[69] Martin Luther King Jr., *Strength to Love* (New York: Harper and Row, 1963), 64.

MY NOTES

MY NOTES

LORD'S PRAYER

OR

Our Father in heaven,
    hallowed be your name,
    your kingdom come,
    your will be done,
        on earth as in heaven.
Give us today our daily bread.
Forgive us our sins
    as we forgive those
        who sin against us.
Save us from the time of trial
    and deliver us from evil.
For the kingdom, the power,
    and the glory are yours,
    now and forever. Amen.

Our Father, who art in heaven,
    hallowed be thy name,
    thy kingdom come,
    thy will be done,
        on earth as it is in heaven.
Give us this day our daily bread;
and forgive us our trespasses,
    as we forgive those
        who trespass against us;
and lead us not into temptation,
    but deliver us from evil.
For thine is the kingdom,
    and the power, and the glory,
    forever and ever. Amen.

PADRE NUESTRO

Padre nuestro que estás en el cielo,
    santificado sea tu nombre.
Venga tu reino.
Hágase tu voluntad
    en la tierra como en el cielo.
Danos hoy nuestro pan de cada día.
Perdona nuestras ofensas
    como también nosotros
        perdonamos a los que nos ofenden.
No nos dejes caer en tentación
    y líbranos del mal.
Porque tuyo es el reino,
    tuyo es el poder y tuya es la gloria,
    ahora y siempre. Amén.